INCLUSIVITY THROUGH A TRANSDISCIPLINARY PRISM

VOLUME - 1

DR. GIFTSY DORCAS E. | DR. SARANYA NARAYANAN | DR. BRIGHTON A. ROSE | DR. NEHA KUMARI

Contents

Contents

Acknowledgements

We owe our deep sense of gratitude to Fr. Dr. Augustine George, Principal, Kristu Jayanti College (Autonomous), Bengaluru, and the management of Kristu Jayanti College (Autonomous), Bengaluru, for providing a platform to exchange academic discourses.

We record our deepest sense of gratitude to Fr. Joshy Mathew, Head, Department of English, Kristu Jayanti College (Autonomous), Bengaluru, for his unfailing support and guidance rendered at every juncture of this venture.

We express our appreciation to Dr. Lyola Thomas, Programme Co-ordinator (PG), Department of English, Kristu Jayanti College (Autonomous), Bengaluru, and Mr. Jerrin Jose, Progrogramme Co-ordinator (UG), Department of English, Kristu Jayanti College (Autonomous), Bengaluru, for their constant support.

We wholeheartedly thank each of the contributing authors for being a part of this book and adding lustre through their proficient research work.

Prologue

"A diverse mix of voices leads to better discussions, decisions, and outcomes for everyone."

~ Sundar Pichai, Chief Executive Officer of Google

Humanity, today, is grappling on the cusp of devastating crises and rapid advancement in every field. In this ever changing and diverse world, the need for inclusivity has never been more critical. Inclusiveness is about accepting and celebrationg differences regardless of ones diverse ethinic backgrounds, identities, or characteristics. Inclusivity, when examined through the lens of a transdiciplinary perspective, aims to develop a holistic understanding of complex problems by integrating knowledge from diverse disciplines. Inclusivity must begin by acknowledging and valuing the diverse perspectives, expertise, and experiences of individuals.

This book is a collection of 22 research papers presented at the Virtual National Conference organised by the Department of English, Kristu Jayanti College (Autonomous), Bengaluru, on the theme *Inclusivity through a Transdisciplinary Prism* held on January 24th & 25th, 2023. The conference resounded the idea of inclusivity ardently reinforced by the United Nations in its 2030 Agenda for Sustainable Development and its Sustainable Development Goals (SDGs). The research papers in this volume contribute to understanding and addressing issues related to diversity, discrimination, and social exclusion. The creative and critical perspectives, and contexts discussed through these works, bridge the gap between theory and practice, as well as between research and implementation, thus connecting us with the common aim to re-examine our actions so as to create a more equitable society where everyone can celebrate their uniqueness.

Preface

Anugraha S. P. and **Dr. Sidney Shirly**, in their paper titled **"Towards a New Paradigm: Cinematographic Literature in English Language Teaching"**, examine the scope of teaching English language through cinematographic literature as a nexus of interrelationship between literature and movies. They focus on how film adaptation is one of the most advantageous multimedia teaching tools that has gained traction in the field of literature.

"Myth or Real: A critical reading on the inclusivity of Gender in Media" is a research paper by **Anupama Murali** and **Thahisn Z. Husain** which investigates whether Gender is really open to all on social media as we believe. The paper attempts to read the reality associated with the inclusion of gender in the media.

Arunima A. V., in her paper titled **"The Embodiment of Eros and Inclusivity: A Study of the Interaction of Bodies in a Classroom"**, explores the concept of Eros. She has emphasied upon the significance of addressing the issues that come with the body. The paper focuses on the differences, discrimination, and exclusivity that characterise pedagogical relationships in an erotically charged classroom.

The paper titled as **"Construing Representation of Queer Characters in Indian Cinema"** by **Bashisha Lizza L.Rani** and **Dr. Ehboklang Pyngrope** explores the narratives given to the characters in select Indian movies that represent the LGBTQA+ community. It dealt with the roles played by the LGBTQ+ characters and their representation in the movies.

"Inclusion of Third Gender: An Analytical Reading of Select Bollywood Films" is a paper by **Bhavya Pahuja**, which presents an explicit portrayal of the trans community in Bollywood films that is either disregarded or has controversial consequences. It also analyses the stereotypes and stigma associated with the third gender roles. The study examined the paradigmatic shift of the portrayal of transgenders from the early times to that of the contemporary period.

C. J. Ginsen's research paper on "**Inclusivity of the Marginalized People of Kerala in the 19th Century: with Special Reference to the Role of Christian Missionaries**", investigates the efforts made by the Christian Missionaries with respect to uplifting the Marginalised People in Kerala. It also presents a study of the educational policies adopted by the Missionaries which brought about the change in social environment there.

Dr. K. C. Lalithambika, in her paper "**A National Inclusive Education Framework to Schools on their Journey towards Inclusion**", presents a detailed study of the comprehensive school atmosphere that ensures that all the students get the opportunity to obtain the essential skills and attitude to be energetic citizen and to be successful at effort and in the social order, which is the line with the education strategy of the Ministry for Education and Employment (MEDE) as stated in the structure for the Education policy for Malta 2014–2024 (MEDE, 2014).

Dr. N. Ravikumar and **Dr. Masilamani C.** in their paper titled "**Inclusive Curriculum Construction and Modern Pedagogies to Enhance the Fundamentals of English Language Skills for English as Second Language Learners**" focus upon the key principles of inclusive curricular design as well as cutting-edge pedagogical techniques for fostering the development of the fundamental language abilities. They discuss the comprehensive curriculum which refers to all of the learning opportunities that students have in school, in the classroom, in the library, and elsewhere, and also, the experiences that students have while taking part in different activities in the classroom, library, lab, workshop, and playground.

In the paper "**The Regressive Effects of Child Abuse and its Constructive Solution through Torey Hayden's One Child**", **Dr. Pauline V. N.** and **Ms. Daffline Gladson** analyse the book One Child by Torey Hayden, which talks about child abuse undergone by a little girl called Sheila which made her violent, and uncooperative eventually leading to maladaptive conduct and mannerisms.

Dr. Pavithra, in her paper **"Inclusion of Theatre as a Pedagogical Tool in Rural Schools"** focuses on teaching through theater and tries to explore theater as a major pedagogical tool in the teaching school curriculum by teachers in the rural sector. The paper works on the observation that the current worldwide environment has significantly altered the scope of theater and its capacity to impart knowledge to students and people with a wide range of skills.

Dr. Sreedevi Santhosh in her paper **"Engendered City Spaces: Functional Marginalities"** explores whether Bengaluru's shift into Bangalore through its cosmopolitan facelift has been better inclusive of the considered categories and if its perception as an exclusively male space has changed. The paper attempts to to mark 'self –construction' in relation to the changing city, evaluating opportunities subject to mobility with its transformation into a hyper-urbanised space, marked by its skyscrapers, metros, ola and uber, swiggy and zomato, media of transit and to explore if it tangentially transforms into zones of safety or if it cramps individuation

In the paper titled "**The Deception of Inclusivity: Challenging the Paradigm of 'Community' in Cults like 'Children of God' and 'Scientology"**, **Josephine Mercy** exposes those cult groups that have secured the hearts of millions across the globe owing to their powerful philosophies, which on thorough investigation, prove to be rooted on sham and trickery. Her paper presents a study of the paradigm of community that is built in those cults and the redeeming power of education that has freed the minds of people from falling deeper into these abysses of chaos.

In the paper titled **"An Exclusive Inclusivity of All Sexual Minorities in Queer Theory: An Exclusive Analysis of Sarah Schulman's Select Novels"**, **Joseph K. J.** and **Dr. J. Amalaveenus** explore inclusion of all sexual minorities in queer theory and the inadequacy and exclusivity of other theories and terms to be inclusive of all sexual inclination in the light of the select novels of queer novelist Sarah Schulman.

J. Revathy and **Dr. Murugavel S.** in their paper titled, **"Rising of popular Literary Devices (Stream of Consciousness) in "The Dark Holds No Terror" by Shashi Deshpande"** attempts a psychological analysis of the novel and makes a comprehensive study of the Stream of Consciousness technique employed by the writer in the narrative.

Padmapriya P. and **Dr.A. Ganesan**'s paper "**Homonationalism: A Theoretical Understanding of Gender and Homonormativity as National Identities in the Select Bollywood Movies**" examines the xenophobic and homophobic notions and picturisation in Bollywood films which helps to trace the historical evolution of Nation and National identities through the lens of Jasbir K Puar's homonationalism. The paper also analyses homonationalist beliefs in Bollywood films as a contributing element to the spread of homonationalism.

K. Siva Madasamy and **Dr V. Chanthiramathi** in their paper titled **"Manumission in the form of The Day in Shadow by Nayantara Sahgal"**, emphasise upon the identity crises of a liberated woman as found in Nayantara Sahgal's novel The Day in Shadow. The research focuses on the challenges faced by divorced women in patriarchal culture, as well as the violent marriage settlement following it, confirming the title's claim that Simrit experiences as a Manumission and identity crisis throughout the work.

"Retelling Mythos in a Green Light: Exploring the Centrifugal Tendency of Select Mythological Retellings" is a paper by **P. Divya** where she explores the way Mythological retellings act as a centrifuge as they move away from the center to focus on the elements that remain on the margins. They seek to include what the center has hitherto excluded. She analyses Kalidasa's Shakuntala and Sujata Bhatt's poems titled "A Different Way to Dance" and "What Happened to the Elephant?" to conclude her point.

"Inclusivity of Modernity in diverse Tribal Culture as reflected in the novel The Stupid Cupid by Mamang Dai" is a research paper by **Preha C.** and **Dr. Crispine Shiny**. Here, they have focused on the major aspects of inclusivity of the modern culture into the diverse culture of tribes. They have studied the change in socio-cultural aspects of tribal culture as reflected in the novel Stupid Cupid by Mamang Dai.

Ramya. B and **Dr. Poonam** in their paper titled **"Spatial and Ethnic Inclusiveness in Gothic Setting: A study in The Silence of the Ghosts by Jonathan Aycliffe and That Frequent Visitor by Hari Kumar K."**, investigate the ethnic inclusion of the representations of family property in The Silence of the Ghosts by Jonathan Aycliffe and That Frequent Visitor by Hari Kumar. The paper emphasises on the ancestral property as a gothic setting that embodies ethnic inclusivity in gothic spatial inclusiveness.

"Deconstructing the gender bias in Amish Tripathi's Ram: The Scion of Ikshvaku and Sita: Warrior of Mithila", a research paper by **R. Lavanya** and **Dr. K.Muthurajan**, examines how the stereotypical portrayals are deconstructed in Amish Tripathi's celebrated novel Ram: The Scion of Ikshvaku and Sita: Warrior of Mithila. They further establish that the narrative style which deconstructs the gender-bias has a wide reach among the reading public.

In a paper titled **"Gender Exclusion to Inclusion: Overcoming Terror with the Power of Self-Defense in Vipin Das's Movie Jaya Jaya Jaya Jaya Hey"**, **Sincy Davis** studies the capacity of women to challenge their oppressors and use physical resistance through martial arts with the support of the latest Malayalam movie, Jaya Jaya Jaya Jaya Hey. The capacity of women to shift their living surroundings from a gender exclusive to a gender-inclusive one with body strength and mind power is also highlighted here.

"The Inclusion of Genderqueer in Malayalam Films Chanthupott and Mumbai Police" is a paper by **SruthiMerin Mathew** wherein she critically looks into the instances in the Malayalam films which incorporates queer community in their narratives. It questions the 'normalising' attitudes often seen in those films which depict the lives of the queer community as an aberration from the 'normal' standards, thereby, throwing some light upon the serious issues faced by the queer community resulting from such 'normalising' attitudes often seen in the Malayalam films.

-Editors

About The Editors

Dr. Giftsy Dorcas E., hails from Tamil Nadu and works as an English faculty at Kristu Jayanti College (Autonomous), Bengaluru. She has completed her doctoral degree in English. Her areas of interest include Emotional Intelligence, Social Emotional Learning (SEL) and Diasporic Writing. She has been a First Rank Holder in her undergraduation, postgratuation and M.Phil. She also holds an MBA degree. A strong believer of God, a writing enthusiast she is a published writer having co-authored a poetry book Word Warriors: A Book of Poetry (2018); compiled 3 anthologies Riparian Reveries (2021), Cakes and Carols (2021) & Red Wine (2021); published poems, short stories in 60 plus anthologies, and has also been part of 7 National Record holding books. She has research publications in 14 journals and 4 chapters in books along with editing a book Pens & Pupils (2023), co-editing 2 books Phonetics Excercise Handbook (2023) and Trending Research Concern (2023). She is a recepient of awards like Young Teacher Award, 2023 given by Research Foundation of India & InkQuill Holders Award, 2022.

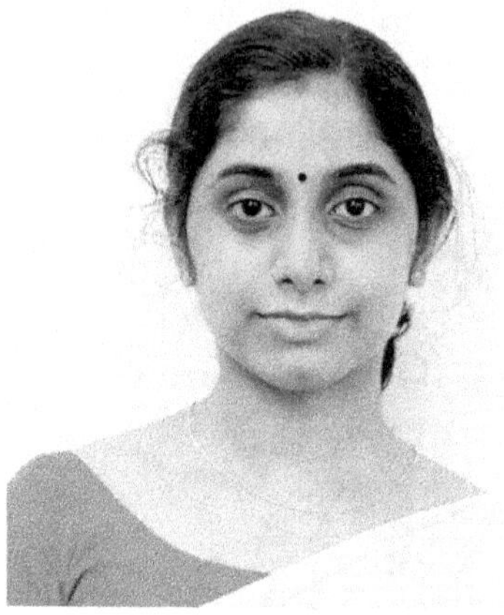

Dr. Saranya Narayanan, is currently an Assistant Professor at the Department of English, Kristu Jayanti College, Bengaluru. She completed her PhD from the Department of English, Amrita Vishwa Vidyapeetham. Her thesis explored the complex ways in which literary narratives represent, depict and engage with traumatic experiences. Her research specialty and interests include Trauma Studies, Gender studies and Women's writing. She has published scholarly articles and book chapters in esteemed academic journals and edited collections, and presented research works at various national and international conferences.

Dr. Brighton A. Rose, is working as an Assistant Professor of English, Kristu Jayanti College (Autonomous), Bengaluru. He has presented papers at the National, International Conferences and also published papers in the national, international journals of repute. He has also delivered talks at the National Seminars, Conferences. His area of specialization includes Subaltern Literature, Postcolonial Literature. He is ardent researcher cum academician who strives for perfection in his academic pursuits.

Dr. Neha Kumari, is currently working as an Assistant Professor of English at Kristu Jayanti College (Autonomous), Bangalore. She pursued her Ph.D. from SKM University, Dumka, Jharkhand, a state government University. She has qualified UGC NET and KSET exams. She started her teaching career in the year 2017. She has around 4.5 years of teaching experience. She has participated in National and International Conferences and presented papers. Her area of interest includes British Literature, American Literature, Children's Literature, and Indian writing in English. Her research topic was "J. K. Rowling: Exploring a New Territory in the Genre of Fiction".

Towards a New Paradigm: Cinematographic Literature in English Language Teaching

Anugraha S. P.[1] and Dr. Sidney Shirly[2]

[1]*Ph.D. Research Scholar, Reg.no: 18213164012001, Department of English & Research Centre, Scott Christian College (Autonomous), Nagercoil- 629003, Tamil Nadu, India.*

[2]*Associate Professor, Department of English & Research Centre, Scott Christian College, (Autonomous), Nagercoil- 629003, Tamil Nadu, India.*

Abstract

This paper examines the scope of teaching English language through cinematographic literature as a nexus of interrelationship between literature and movies. A critical outlook at the 21st century of English language teaching has exposed the fact that various outputs have been made through digital aesthetics. The film adaptation is one of the most advantageous multimedia teaching tools that has gained traction in the field of literature. The objective behind this study is to make known the potential of cinematographic literature in enhancing motivation of students, interest in the literature programme, and stimulating their ability to comprehend literary adaptations in language teaching. Besides, this paper aims to provide teachers with a foundation for creative, updated, and, perhaps, effective language teaching using cinematographic literature.

Keywords: Cinematographic literature, Language acquisition, Languaculture.

Introduction

Cinematographic literature is the medium of teaching and learning authentic language. It seeks to build bridges between print textuality and multimedia technologies, literature and movies. Literature is an art which is developed through writings while movies bring those writings to life through sound, colour, music, visuals and motion. Movies are literature; adaptations are the result of a beautiful association between literary works and technology. This idea of building bridges between print and screen literature is a useful starting point to teach and learn English language through literary adaptations. The inclusion of cinematographic literature fosters the development of the macro skills of communication (reading, listening, writing, and speaking), critical and creative thinking, digital literacy, being a motivating tool that suits students' preferences, being appropriate for their learning and language style, pronunciation, promoting their understanding of the texts' content, and giving them an authentic exposure to languaculture.

Why Cinematographic Literature in ELT?

English, a lingua franca in the country, has attained a status much higher than the Indian languages. In spite of this being the medium of instruction for many students in the country, the language still eludes many of them. There are many new approaches coming up to address the challenges and make the language learning easier for students but the stark reality remains the same or rather gets worse day by day. While language learning through technology is highly discussed and recommended on one side, the current language classrooms present a bleak picture of insufficiency in terms of efforts to actualize the already existing methodologies and also insist on bringing out more practical approaches to English language teaching.

Building bridges between print and screen literature is necessary because of the traditional approaches to language learning and teaching, which emphasize a teacher-centered environment, the 'chalk and talk' method, and the use of text-based instructional materials. The instructor is typically the one in complete control of the teaching process and is regarded as the only source of knowledge. In a classroom setting, lectures are delivered to the students, who are massively spoon-fed with large loads of textual information. As an alternative, cinematographic literature in ELT was developed in part as an effort to restructure language communication. It is intended to interact with its viewers and users using a range of modes and tools, indicating a clear break from the conventional fixation with novelty. The use of cinematographic literature in English classes encourages students to learn languages naturally and creatively. Also, engagement and cooperation between students as well as between students and teachers are key components of the language acquisition process. It is commonly believed that students dislike taking an active role in the learning process and prefer to accept the teacher's material as gospel. It might be able to solve this issue by providing an innovative, student-centered environment. In this sense, cinematographic literature functions efficiently in English classrooms wherein students can reconstruct their knowledge collaboratively and also meet their needs. Additionally, because they are used to a variety of audio-visual technology outside of the classroom, students generally accept the use of film adaptations as a teaching tool. Students are empowered in this setting and can take an active role in their learning process.

Merits of Cinematographic Literature in ELT

Cinematogrphic literature has the potential to communicate with both the print and screen version, and this results in double exposure to the students in the combination of literature and films. The true essence of language learning is acquired when both the print and screen literature are made use of together. The language of print literature is well organized by the wonderful choice of diction. The language used in screen literature, however, offers a genuine source of actual language. Despite being scripted, it is asserted that cinema dialogues mimic real spoken language, which makes up the majority of native-like speech. Students' perceived levels of proficiency may rise if teachers help them learn terms from the language they will use in everyday life. As a multimodal tool, cinematographic literature helps students understand what they are consuming by allowing them to concurrently listen to language exchanges and see the body language and paralanguage of communication, such as facial expressions, voice tone, and gestures. These visual cues serve to draw attention to the verbal message and reinforce it. Additionally, it contextualizes the spoken word in a visual and aural manner, which identifies additional viewpoints for language understanding. Above all, cinematographic literature overcomes the limitations of traditional approaches and calls for a much broader view of literacy with multimodality.

Cinematographic Literature and Languaculture

Language generally represents culture, and both are intertwined. However, students ignore people, the setting, and culture when they consider language learning. They believe that language is a static, closed, and conventional set of words and grammar rules that necessitates extensive memorization. Language acquisition includes not only grammar and vocabulary, but also learning cultural features, habits and behaviours along with living conditions. According to Agar, "The *langua* in languaculture is about discourse, not just about words and sentences. And the *culture* in languaculture is about meanings that include, but go well beyond, what the dictionary and the grammar offer" (96). When teaching or learning a language, it is of paramount importance to refer to the culture where the language belongs to, because language is deep-rooted in culture. In order to grasp the language itself and use it effectively, language learners must be aware of the cultural elements ingrained in the target language.

Cinematographic literature offers students a chance to witness people, the context and culture that are not apparent in the traditional classrooms. Furthermore, there are extensive techniques to encapsulate a wide range of intricate cultural components, such as values, beliefs, customs and behaviours. It can also increase students' intercultural understanding. The use of films is also praised by Herron et al. because they are effective tools that can aid in "depicting the foreign language culture more effectively than other instructional materials" (518). Using film adaptations in a classroom setting, not only makes students learn more about the diversity of the target language culture, but also to understand the language of the native speakers. Although literary works typically tell fictional stories with concocted settings, characters, and actions, they frequently highlight significant elements of a real society, giving students a window into the distinctive cultural traits of a target language environment and allowing them to draw comparisons and contrasts with their own life, society, and beliefs. As literature and films have become the mirror of society due to the unique reflection of culture, language learning becomes much easier and superior with cinematographic literature. It frequently speaks to various students with various expectations and knowledge. This helps to understand how both the media are cross pollinated and subsequently create a new body of work that is unique in nature to upgrade the language learning process.

Cinematographic Literature and Learning Style

The necessity to keep up with technology developments and the desire to take into account the learning preferences of contemporary students may drive the design of a more innovative, student-centered environment. Students learn in diversified ways, by visualizing, hearing, memorizing and reflecting. The biggest difficulty facing education today is how to teach a population that is growing up in the digital era to instructors who are digital immigrants. Prensky asserts that "digital natives" learn differently from "digital immigrants" because they were raised in the digital era (2). He claims, "Digital Natives are used to receiving information really fast. They like to parallel process and multi-task. They prefer their graphics before their text rather than the opposite. They prefer random access (like hypertext). They function best when networked" (2). Furthermore, Kuzma et al. posit, "We teach and live in a culture dominated by film, television, and other visual media. Our students . . . spend a major portion of their time in front of the television, at the computer, or in a movie theater. Consequently, they are geared to audiovisual rather than written forms of expression and communication" (34). Accordingly, cinematographic literature as an effective multimodal tool resides in the fact that it is highly suitable for the contemporary educational context.

Cinematographic literature can add flexibility and variety to the language classroom by enhancing the range of teaching resources and methods and by assisting students in growing their communication competence. An entire film adaptation or sequence, for example, can be utilized as practise for speaking and writing as well as a model for listening and reading. Utilizing film adaptations in specific task activities is a great way to promote active teaching and learning while also getting students involved and interacting with one another. Additionally, it can serve as a real catalyst for student participation in class discussions by eliciting diverse viewpoints on social issues and reviving a discourse. By showing various literary adaptations, it is also possible to add more variety to language classes. Its flexible application enables a variety of classroom learning experiences for the students. Cinematographic literature serves as a vehicle that can further increase students' motivation in this regard.

Cinematographic Literature and Pronunciation

Pronunciation is more than listening and repeating, as is usually taught in the traditional classrooms. It includes features of language and communication skills. Hornby states that "pronunciation is the way in which a language is spoken, the way in which a word is pronounced, the way a person speaks the words of a language" (928). In this sense, pronunciation refers to how a word or language is said. However, many words in the English language are spoken differently by different individuals, depending on various factors such as, the region in which they grow up, their socioeconomic status, their ethnic group, their previous education, etc.

Accordingly, Brown claims "movie is the most widely applicable and powerful among the resources for teaching and learning since it has unique capacity to communicate, to influence, and to inform" (233). Concentrating on sounds in the screen version of the text makes the students aware of the spoken language and provides them extra information about the paralinguistic features of communication such as volume of voice, speed of voice, pronunciation, intonation, tone, articulation, pause, etc. which assist them in achieving the goal of better understanding on pronunciation. Besides, when students view the screen version of the text directly, they acquire both pictorial and auditory representation and it influences their understanding and thinking capacity. The use of cinematographic literature in the classroom helps students acquire the English language by simulating how a native speaker would pronounce words, and uses the body language while speaking. Moreover, it involves listening to how the words, phrases and sentences of a language sounds and practicing by focusing on connected speech while playing sequences from the screen version of the text. Therefore, cinematographic literature encourages language learning practices with intelligibility and communication activities.

Sample Language Activities:

The session involves students watching twenty minutes or more of a scene from the screen version of the literary text in the target language (English). Language activities are given to the students to work at various levels (collaboratively or individually) in response to the scene.

Tasks	Activities
Gap filling	Completing dialogues by choosing words or sentences that best fits each gap.
Arranging and sorting	Arranging the dialogues according to the scene.
Compare and Contrast	Analyze the differences between the scene in the print and screen versions.
Problem-solving	Prediction sharing (What happened before and after the selected scene). Detective play (investigate to determine genre, place, time, mood found in the selected scene.
Sharing Experiences	Talk about the most or least favourite characters, scenes and location.
Creativity and Imagination	Screen adaptation review (podcast, video, oral, written). Retell a scene from a different perspective. Replace or bring about change in a particular character. Role-play or re-enactment of a scene (groups or individual). Discuss alternative endings. Highlight key issues and themes in the scene. Develop a story about a secondary character.

Conclusion

Cinematographic literature attempts to dismantle the once commonplace view that print and screen literature are opposed to one another. It demonstrates that there exists a recursive relationship between literature and film, and that when viewed in terms of continuity, not rupture; one is able to get the understanding of the other. Screen literature can and should be understood not in opposition to print literature, but in the light of it.

Literary adaptations, which were initially made for entertainment purposes, include pedagogical value that might make them worthwhile to employ in the context of education and language learning. Using screen versions of the literary works enhances the students' communication, pronunciation, motivation, non-verbal components of communication, cross-cultural comparison and provides them different ways of input. It gives students the chance to experience the people, traditions, and cultures of the target language group. Moreover, cinematographic literature as a multimodal tool has been designed to meet the learning needs of the contemporary students to allow them to navigate and comprehend the different modes of communication. It also provides English classrooms with a more valuable teaching and learning process by bringing forth a more flexible, integrated, student-centered, experiential, and of course, an enjoyable environment.

References

- Agar, Michael H. *Language Shock: Understanding The Culture of Conversation.* New
- York, William Morrow P, 1994.
- Brown, Douglas H. *Language Assessment Principles and Classroom Practices.* London,
- Longman P, 2004.
- Herron, Carol, et al. "The Effectiveness of a Video-Based Curriculum in Teaching

- Culture." *The Modern Language Journal*, vol. 83, no. 4, 1999, pp. 518–33. *JSTOR*, www.jstor.org/stable/330523.
- Hornby, Albert Sydney. *Oxford Advanced Learner's Dictionary*. Great Britain, Oxford UP,
- 1995.
- Kuzma, Lynn M., and Patrick J. Haney. "And ... Action! Using Film to Learn about Foreign
- Policy." *International Studies Perspectives*, vol. 2, no. 1, Feb. 2001, pp. 33-50, doi:10.1111/1528-3577.00036.
- Prensky, Marc. "Digital Natives, Digital Immigrants." *On the Horizon,* vol. 9, no. 5, MCB
- UP, Sept. 2001, pp. 1-6, doi:10.1108/10748120110424816.

---

[1]**Anugraha S. P.,** is a full time Research Scholar, Department of English,Scott Christian College (Autonomous), Nagercoil which is affiliated to Manonmaniam Sundaranar University, Abishekapatti, Tirunelveli, Tamil Nadu, India. Her Research interests include English Language Teaching, Literature and Film Studies and Comparative Literature.

[2]**Dr. Sidney Shirly,** works as an Associate Professor of English Scott Christian College (Autonomous), Nagercoil. Her area of interest is Commonwealth Literature.

• • •

Myth or Real: A Critical Reading on the Inclusivity of Gender in Media

Anupama Murali[1] and Thahisn Z. Husain[2]

[1]Assistant Professor, Department of English, MES Ponnani College, Ponnani Malappuram, Kerala

[2]Assistant Professor, Department of English, MES Ponnani College, Ponnani Malappuram, Kerala.Kerala

Abstract

Is the term Gender really open to all on the social media as we believe? It seems all inclusive but one eventually realise that it is a deceptive one. The internet psyche has been conditioned in such a way that the inclusion is strictly confined to those who express and exhibit oneself adhering to unwritten parameters. For example there is no room for dissent when it comes to accepting the standards of beauty constricting the concept of beauty to "white, fair and lean". A majority of the internet population is still biased on what it reads and sees. Gender is in itself is a huge umbrella term which includes all sorts of human beings, but the media is hesitant towards assimilating the greater idea of Gender and narrow it down to a fewer privileged classes, men with power, white woman etc. The prejudice towards 'other' which does not fit into the so called" conformist" category is explicit and it goes to such an extent where it virtually kills the 'other'. The normality spins around white centred attitude, brands, and publications with little space and voice for the minority. The paper attempts to read the reality associated with the inclusion of gender in media. Is it for real or a myth? Whether the reality or truth we see today is an illusory truth effect of ideologies and truth propagated by those in power.

Keywords: Gender, media, other, myth, deception, truth

Gender is not a biological construct; rather, it is created by society and individuals. As a result, attitudes toward gender are always changing and can vary greatly across cultures, nations, and generations. The term "gender" describes how society views the various roles, expectations, and relationships between men and women. Depending on social and cultural situations, men and women hold different positions and have different expectations of what is masculine and feminine. Gender dictates what behaviour is acceptable, expected, and valued in a woman or a man in a particular situation. For instance, in many countries, women are more frequently expected to take care of the home and raise the children, while males are more frequently under financial strain. The perception of women is as sensitive and caring while men are perceived as strong. The study of gender and the intersections of gender with other categories of identity, such as ethnicity, sexuality, class, and nationality, is done through the interdisciplinary field of gender studies. It works to advance gender equality and combat prejudice against women and other underrepresented groups. Traditional ideas about sex and gender are frequently questioned in gender studies. It's pretty depressing to see how the mainstream social media perpetuates the idea of gender, even in the era of gender studies and the LGBTQA+ movements. It continues to support gender stereotypes and centre on the binary "normative" concept of gender.

Through advertising and images showing women in a variety of jobs, from caring for children to working, the media promote gender roles and behavioural tendencies in women while portraying males as more independent and less inclined to show emotion. Therefore, although while the digital world gives us the opportunity to express ourselves through our e-identities, in reality, digital settings just serve to mimic the gender norms and culture that are already present in the physical world.

In addition to providing information and entertainment, media also has an impact on people's lives through influencing their opinions, attitudes, and behaviours. By quietly expressing the dominant hegemonic worldview, it manipulates social behaviours. By elevating men's dominance over women, society has institutionalised male hegemony in terms of gender representation. Stereotypical representations of masculinity and femininity are at the centre of gendered representation in media worldwide. The notions of masculinity and femininity are products of culture and represent the socially sanctioned distinctions between men and women. Gender stereotypes and social media have an impact on how people view women's bodies. Images of feminine attractiveness and specific role models are promoted by the media. The prevailing societal assumptions regarding the aesthetics of body image still exist. Due to gender norms, women who post online are subjected to harassment in which they are harshly criticised for both their appearance and their content. The prevalence of misogynistic content, reports of shadow banning or violence against women online, and other factors make it obvious that some online areas are breeding grounds for divisive political views and behaviour. These forces frequently leave little place for non-heteronormative sexualities or people's experiences of gender outside of the binary, with the tendency to reinforce existing gender standards. This is seen by the ongoing availability of offensive material aimed at women and other non-conforming genders on these sites. Our interactions with gender norms are being shaped by social media, often in sexist, racist, and discriminatory ways.

Women are underrepresented in media representations of gender, which implies wrongly that men set societal norms and that women are inconsequential or invisible. Then, men and women are depicted in ways that reinforce stereotyped conceptions of gender that are supported by society. The portrayals of male and female interactions place a focus on conventional roles and normalise violence against women. In social media, the broader concept of gender is invisible. Gender is never extended beyond the binary notion of normativity.

The media frequently portrays men and women in unequal ways. The biggest sources of gender stereotyping are the advertisements that emerge on social media. In social media advertisements, women are frequently portrayed as sex objects. While men's advertisements typically highlight cars, business products, or investments, women are more frequently depicted in commercials for cosmetic and home goods. The fact that advertising usually feature entire images of women and close-ups of men is another crucial factor. The female body is objectified when seen in its whole, whereas partial views create favourable feelings. Advertisements typically show men and women in accordance with predetermined notions of femininity and masculinity. Being a male is being masculine, while being a woman is being feminine. With the exception of specialty marketing, there isn't much potential for variation or role-reversals. In contrast to their male counterparts, female characters continue to exhibit significantly more flesh, as well as exceedingly small waists and other exaggerated body components. Instilling unrealistic body ideals in very young children as a result of the hypersexualization and objectification of female characters helps to reinforce unfavourable body perceptions and images during the formative years. The media frequently disparages males who take up caring or household responsibilities or who reject violence. Similar descriptions have the eventuality to change generalizations of what society may anticipate of men and women, as well as what those individualities may anticipate from themselves. There was a time when the media vehemently promoted lean and fair women as successful in their lives and career. It was an indirect scathing attack on the morale and confidence of the talented Indian skin. One can easily assume how those soaps would have affected the budding roses to fallupon the thorns of 'colour'. Over the years attitudes and conceptions changed and definition of Beauty has new parameters.

But how far we have come forward in terms of gender inclusivity in media? A recent incident calls for a close introspection. Recently Instagram asked a woman to remove their photos on the charges that it was obscene. The so called obscenity was nothing but her obese body and a dark skin tone. At the same time the platform encourages nudity almost when they are exposed by the fair complexion. They advocate for an uneven view of what men and women should play in society. As a result, social media and traditional media both continue to reflect culturally defined gender norms and relationships.

Even after many years of movements and protests, the societal roles and position of woman is still stereotyped. The social media reinforces the stereotypical role of man and woman. Along with woman, people who belong to varied gender identities also share the marginalised and condemned position in the social media space. It is true that social media made Trans - people visible, but it also made them vulnerable. In the beginning, the internet created a means for transgender individuals to communicate with one another swiftly and across great distances. Since then, social media and YouTube have used Trans people's visibility to significantly advance policy. The emergence of Tumblr and YouTube gave Trans individuals, the ability to become independent content producers, bypassing the cis media gatekeepers who had previously controlled how Trans people were viewed in society. But with the advancement there came the conservative opposition and initiatives to deny their fundamental human rights. The conformist group is instigating the backlash among conservatives. They employ social media and any other online forums for anti-trans propagandists who share a common goal of propagating false information. Most frequently Trans individuals are the target of online harassment on social media. Any Trans person who receives public attention, even for non-trans related news items, has to face a surge of online abuse in return. Media has a responsibility to not just treat Trans people with dignity, but also to give accurate information. But usually what happens is that the anti-trans people conversations are extremely visible and it is very often factually incorrect. Social media is now the battleground on which the marginalised gender fights against hate, against intolerance, against disinformation. Online bullying mainly targets transgender people using social media. Any trans person who is the subject of media attention—even for stories that are not specifically about trans people—must deal with an increase in online harassment in return. Media must not just treat transgender individuals with respect but also provide accurate information. The dialogues that are hostile to transgender persons, however, are typically highly public and frequently false. The marginalised gender now battles against hate, prejudice, and misinformation on the social media frontlines.

Social media are widely used in society and play a significant role in how each individual views others. But in doing so, these media reinforce the warped and conventional gender and racial stereotypes of a patriarchal society and aid in ingraining them in the minds of young people at a juvenile age, which could have extremely negative effects. Different cultural groups are severely underrepresented and ignored in these platforms. By stereotyping specific groups and painting a false picture of different groupings, social media also plays a bigger part in forming collective identities and intergroup attitudes. Certain social and cultural groupings are depicted negatively and unrealistically as a result of its strong hold on people's attitudes and ability to shape up their ideas.

The digital era restated and reemphasized various prejudices and presuppositions regarding women and other marginalised gender emphasising their second gender status. Difficulties in distancing from associated gender roles even in the postmodern democratic social constructs could be seen as a perfect example of the negative consequence of adhering to stereotypes. The primary role of women as home makers and men as providers is prophesized across the social media, despite the progress society has achieved in dilating the divisions in gender roles and overlook the fact that gender role is ever evolving .Societal norms are particular in maintaining hetero normativity and ousting the 'other' genders. Even today, regardless of the fact that people are so much more conscious of the issue, social media still perpetuates traditional gender standardization and keeps on voicing the perspectives from a patriarchal view point.

References

- Butler, Judith. Gender Trouble: Feminism and the Subversion of Identity. Routledge, Taylor & Francis Group, 2015.
- Butler, Judith. Undoing Gender. Routledge, 2004.
- Devine, Patricia G. "Stereotypes and prejudice: Their automatic and controlled components." Journal of Personality and Social Psychology 56.1 (1989).
- Duffy, B. E., & Pruchniewska, U. (2012). Gender and Entrepreneurialism in the Social Media Age: A Digital Double Bind.
- Perloff, R. M. (2014). Social media effects on young women's body image concerns: Theoretical perspectives and an agenda for research. Sex roles, 71(11), 363-377.
- Rose, J., Mackey-Kallis, S., Shyles, L., Barry, K., Biagini, D., Hart, C., & Jack, L. (2012). Face it: The impact of gender on social media images. Communication Quarterly, 60(5), 588-607.
- Webb, et al. "Social Media and Gender Issues." ResearchGate, 2015, www.researchgate.net /publication/ 297056278_Social_Media_and_Gender_Issues.

---

[1]**Anupama Murali,** is working as Assistant Professor in the Department of English, MES Ponnani College,Ponnani

Malappuram, Kerala.Her area of interest is cultural studies and gender studies.

[2]**Thahsin Z.Husain,** isworking as Assistant Professor in the Department of English, MES Ponnani College,Ponnani Malappuram, Kerala.Kerala.Her area of interest is ELT and gender studies.

• • •

The Embodiment of Eros and Inclusivity: A Study of the Interaction of Bodies in a Classroom.

Arunima A. V.

Research Scholar, English Literature English and Foreign Languages University, Hyderabad

Abstract

The disregard for the body in a classroom has been problematised by Bell Hooks in many of her works. Acknowledging the presence of bodies demands recognition of eros. Eros is a driving force in a classroom, despite many attempts to discard or ignore it, it reasserts its role through our bodies. Erotic desire fuels the quest for knowledge, that is., the desire for the other and the desire to be whole. This is desirable in a classroom and facilitates a passionate learning experience. However, eros can also be a distracting force in a classroom, especially between teachers and students. Special bonds formed between them pose many challenges as human beings have preferences and are lenient towards physically and emotionally appealing people. Eros is not only about sexual relationships, it is a vital force that ignites the fire of curiosity and love towards learning. However, interactions both sexual and nonsexual bring inequalities and favouritism with them to classroom space. Therefore, this paper is an attempt to emphasize the significance of addressing the issues that come with the body. It focuses on the differences, discrimination, and exclusivity that characterize pedagogical relationships in an erotically charged classroom.

Keywords: Body, Eros, Pedagogy, Classroom, Inclusivity, Appearance, Desire, Passion. Introduction

---

Conventional classroom space in the popular imagination is always a place for the interaction of minds, where the teacher is the provider and the students are the receivers. However, this notion has not escaped objections and some discourses fundamentally problematize the disregard for bodies in a classroom. The duality of the mind and body has been a disputed concept for a long time. Cognitive science proposes the idea of embodied cognition which says "the body or the body's interactions with the environment constitute or contribute to cognition" (Shapiro and Spaulding) Thus, with the changing understanding of mind, the duality is problematized and therefore, the boundary between body and mind is blurred. However, regardless of this concept of embodied cognition, the body is still valid in a classroom for the emotional element that comes with every individual. Bell Hooks emphasizes the significance of being whole in a classroom rather than being a disembodied spirit, thus, validating the presence of eros. According to Schroeder, "Eros, in the broad sense, is not confined to the erotics of sexuality but is that which infuses life into all our partnerships and interactions. Eros is in the partnership of ourselves and creation, between one person and another, between colleagues, students, friends, lovers, and ultimately in relation to our own selves. Eros is the life force." (13)

Eros necessitates an acknowledgement of the presence of the body and its repercussions in a classroom. The power dynamics in a classroom also depend upon erotic passion. The passion or desire for knowledge and the passion for a vitally enriching learning environment which abounds with love are not mutually exclusive. Passion, desire and emotions stem from the body. Therefore, it is imperative to acknowledge that bodies are interacting in a classroom and cognition is also through bodies. The presence of bodies and the consequent emotions can create hierarchies and an imbalance. Hence, they have the potential to challenge the existence of an ideal, all-inclusive classroom space. Thus, this paper attempts to look at the challenges to realizing an inclusive classroom fuelled by erotic passion based on Bell Hooks' essay, "Eros, Eroticism, and the Pedagogical Process".

The Inescapable Body

Bell Hooks says that people enter the classroom determined to erase the body and give themselves over more fully to the mind, consequently, they establish that passion has no place in a classroom. However, passion is there inside everyone but, they are forced to repress it and this results in seeking passion in other private spaces, outside class. (Hooks, 59) The primary contention that she has is with the erasure of the body. She explicates how the concept of the body is obliterated to not influence cognitive functions performed by the quintessential mind. Tina S. Kazan in her essay "Dancing Bodies in the Classroom: Moving toward an Embodied Pedagogy" elaborates how acknowledging his or her body is inevitable in a classroom as a teacher. She says,

Focusing on who we teach and where we teach requires a physical attention to the classroom to better facilitate how we teach. In any given space, a teacher must determine what arrangements and what position(s) for herself make sense for a given class activity. In other words, seeing myself as a body in a space with other bodies enables me to more fully engage in situated practice and to model it for students. While it can be easy to forget that we are bodies in the classroom, such an oversight never lasts long. The wonderful thing about our bodies is that they "betray" us, meaning they remind us at what are sometimes the least opportune moments that we are not only "minds" or "thinkers" in the classroom. As a teaching body, I sneeze and hiccup. I get things caught in my contact lenses. I grow hungry and hear the sounds my stomach generates (loud enough for nearby students to hear), and sometimes I recognize too late, as my heart rate quickens and my hands seem less steady, that I should have refrained from another cup of coffee during office hours. Bodies do not let us pass as minds only, and they may or may not allow us to pass in the ways that we intend. Whether my body enables me to pass as a teaching body or not (as evidenced in my opening scenario) will depend on the other bodies and context(s) involved. (404)

Hence, the body is inescapable even in a classroom regardless of the effort one makes to come across only as the mind. The body gives signals to attend to its needs which cannot be ignored. This applies both to teachers and students, therefore, rather than ignoring the body, it is imperative to adjudicate and look at ways through which we can navigate as bodies in a classroom. It is at this juncture that eros becomes significant as it emerges from the body naturally in a classroom space.

Eros and Pedagogy

Karsten Kenklies in his essay, "The Struggle to Love: Pedagogical Eros and the Gift of Transformation", says that any pedagogical relationship should ideally be based on passionate love and mutual affirmation. In such a relationship, a teacher is not a means to an end for the student and the student looks for safety, guidance, love and recognition for the individual that he or she is. There is an attraction between the teacher and the student and the teacher sees the individual as full of determination and passion and thus, is incentivised to nurture growth and nourish a new life. The teacher's motive is not to fill the student with his or her ideas, concepts or values but to guide and facilitate learning through the motivation that is maintained through mutual attraction. The student and the teacher need to accept each other as a whole being who is mature enough to explore on one's own. (Kenklies, 551)

Kenklies presents eros as a force that kindles learning and has a positive influence on the pedagogical process. According to him, both the teacher and the student benefit from this relationship. Desire fundamentally governs the education process. According to Pryer, teaching and learning are erotic acts, eros is a chaotic flow that is catalyzed by desire. The erotic process is never complete and therefore there is a lack. (82) This lack necessitates a desire for the 'other' to become whole again but it is unattainable and thus remains incomplete. Therefore, desire is frustrating but it drives people to seek knowledge. (Leggo, 236) Hence, it becomes a fruitful experience even though it is unsettling to accept that something is unknown and needs to be learned. There is a constant flux between the space of ignorance and the space of knowledge that expands with the more one acquires. Pryer emphasizes that "The processes of teaching and learning involve the ecstatic abandonment of self to the Other, the continual losing and finding of self in the Other, the intimate, sensual engagement of self with the world." (86) The other is the teacher in a classroom scenario, a doorway to the world. This passion that nurtures an erotic relationship between the teacher and the students is a desirable quality in the pedagogical process. Nonetheless, it is a hugely demanding process to establish such kinds of relationships. Bell Hooks in one of her essays titled "Ecstasy" proposes the concept of 'engaged pedagogy' where the teachers spend quality time with students to understand them and provide specialized teaching finely tuned for the students. A relationship charged with passion facilitates this kind of teaching and eros realizes its full potential in such a class. Thus, eros invigorates a class by paying attention to bodily desire and passion.

However, this process is tiresome as it is impossible to give special attention to each student, especially in a large classroom. This time-consuming exercise fails to be an inclusive endeavour in a practical sense. Consequently, the classroom becomes a space where discrimination flourishes. Bell Hooks says,

Teachers who love students and are loved by them are still "suspect" in the academy. Some of the suspicion is that the presence of feelings, of passions, may not allow for objective consideration of each student's merit. But this very notion is based on the false assumption that education is neutral, that there is some "even" emotional ground we stand on that enables us to treat everyone equally, dispassionately. In reality, special bonds between professors and students have always existed, but traditionally they have been exclusive rather than inclusive. To allow one's feeling of care and will to nurture particular individuals in the classroom—to expand and embrace everyone—goes against the notion of privatized passion. (63)

These special bonds make a way for discrimination and exclusivity. Such bonds can be either sexual or nonsexual, in both these cases, favouritism is inevitable.

In addition to these special relationships, mere attraction -which is subliminal- based on appearances can also lead to discrimination. When the body comes into the picture there are so many facets of that experience that should be taken into account. One of them is the role of physical appearances in classroom power dynamics. The body being the primary focus of this paper, it is crucial to take into account its implications. Apart from bodily needs, the body also stands for aesthetic appeal. This gives rise to a kind of attraction which creates special preferences among students and teachers. The resultant discrimination is not peculiar to a classroom, it is similar to that in the outer world. Appearances, gender, sexuality, race and skin colour are intrinsic aspects of the body that become a part of the classroom power dynamics. When the body is a marker of identity, personal prejudices and preferences get reflected in the relationships and will determine the course of pedagogy. Body image issues hinder the development of a confident self and discrimination gets accentuated by different physical appearances. Eros starts with an acknowledgement of bodily interactions and there is a natural tendency to get attracted to physically appealing people. Teachers and students dedicate some time to making themselves appear presentable in a classroom. They express their identity and individuality through their bodies. The body is a marker that distinguishes between individuals, especially between teachers and students. A teacher should supposedly present himself or herself in a way that is distinct from the students to establish superiority and gain respect. However, these stereotypical notions are always under negotiation and people topple these rules.

Nevertheless, stereotypes are also a matter of concern for students who are also expected to look a certain way. Teachers might prefer certain students based on their physical appearance and vice versa. This implies that there cannot be an equal distribution of love. Thus, physical appearance is a major reason for discrimination and favouritism which are consequences of bodily presence.

This poses a major challenge to realizing an all-inclusive classroom. Despite these attractions and preferences, Bell Hooks makes us think that the same love can be extended to everyone in a classroom without partiality. She says,

In student journals from various classes I have taught there have always been complaints about the perceived special bonding between myself and particular students. Realizing that my students were uncertain about expressions of care and love in the classroom, I found it necessary to teach on the subject. I asked students once: "Why do you feel that the regard I extend to a particular student cannot also be extended to each of you? Why do you think there is not enough love or care to go around?" To answer these questions they had to think deeply about the society we live in, how we are taught to compete with one another. They had to think about capitalism and how it informs the way we think about love and care, the way we live in our bodies, the way we try to separate mind from body. (63)

Hooks asserts that it is possible to extend the same love to everyone and there is no place for competition. This is, however, far from true since she contradicts herself in her essay "Ecstacy" in which she says a large class will undermine "engaged pedagogy". Indicating that with the number of students increasing there develops rivalry, and competition becomes a natural outcome. Hence, it is evident that it is impractical to expect an equal distribution of love in a classroom with more students. However, irrespective of the strength of the class there will be an intervention by personal preferences and prejudices that hamper the formation of an inclusive classroom.

The Sexual Aspect

In addition to attractions and preferences, there are romantic and sexual relationships that flourish especially between students and teachers. Bell Hooks states in her essay, " Passionate Pedagogy: EroticStudent/ Faculty Relationships" that there is always a possibility of erotic longings in a pedagogical relationship. The devotion and passion between a student and teacher have the potential to kindle sexual energy. This is inevitable and cannot be outlawed. It demands recognition and has to be dealt with maturely. Thus, it necessitates us to utilize this erotic energy constructively in a classroom. It requires us to be vigilant so that exploitation and abuse, consequences of such relationships can be unrooted. However, these passionate relationships can also be enabling and positively transforming. Acknowledging the presence of sexual relationships between teachers and students will induce accountability and responsibility. Therefore, issues such as hierarchical exploitation can be addressed. Hence, banning erotic energy will lead to power structures that enable coercion and exploitation to work in secrecy, because it is inevitable, and it is prudent if it can be addressed and used to excite the passion for learning. (50) Thus, Hooks asserts that as long as there is no hierarchy and oppression, erotic relationships between teachers and students are positively stimulating and conducive to the learning experience. She advocates the normalization of such relationships to single out the discrepant and abusive ones. However, this will foster inequality with special relationships between particular teachers and students. This will augment the competition and the solution that Fraser and Garvin give in their essay, "Erotic pedagogy: a student's and professor's perspectives" is that, "in practical terms, embracing erotic pedagogy will require both students and professors to embrace polyamory (that is, the love of many partners). The fact that an instructor may love many students (as well as perhaps a primary partner) and a student may love many professors, requires us to allow for many loves, many deep relationships, simultaneously." (8)

Thus, multiple relationships with an equal preference for everyone is the implied solution which is impractical as it will distract the students and teachers from the actual purpose of the classroom, which is education. This is a utopian vision which is not conducive to an inclusive space as multiple relationships also have the potential to be partial and are time-consuming. Conclusion

Eros is a driving force in a classroom, despite many attempts to discard or ignore it, it reasserts its role through our bodies. Erotic desire fuels the quest for knowledge, that is., the desire for the other and the desire to be whole. This is advisable in a classroom and it facilitates a passionate learning experience. However, eros can also be a distracting force in a classroom, especially between teachers and students. Special bonds formed between them pose many challenges as human beings have preferences and are lenient towards physically and emotionally appealing people. Eros is not only about sexual relationships, it is a fundamental force that ignites the fire of curiosity and love towards learning. However, it is imperative to acknowledge the occurrence of sexual relationships in this context to address the issues of discrimination that arise with them. Kerry Burch says the following about a classroom in which eros is absent.

In this classroom, colored grey, there is no sharing of oneself with others by either the students or the teacher: education, in other words, is a solipsistic affair......There is, however, a significant degree of Order in this classroom. Every body appears to know their place in the undiscussed hierarchy. The teacher, unwaveringly Objective, actively encourages students not to ask any questions about the structure of power within the classroom or the basis of his real or imagined authority. The rows of desks remain in neat, straight lines. Although this space is filled with individual souls, the absence of eros and a shared vision of the good (however the good is envisioned and contested) means the classroom experience is defined by its soullessness. (Burch, 126)

Therefore, eros is a vital force that makes a classroom lively. Eros is an indispensable element in a classroom hence, erasing the body is impossible. Everything is through bodies, from cognition to emotions, and the reverberations of bodily energy are palpable in a classroom. Therefore, the first step towards making a class inclusive is to acknowledge the presence of bodies and eros to address the challenges posed by them. The objective must be to tame the erotic energy and transform it productively.

An inclusive classroom is a utopian ideal towards which the academic members should work. Consistent effort to attain this ideal, inclusive space should be the aim of academia. Practising and maintaining healthy erotic relationships are essential to attain inclusivity. Eros makes a classroom a highly competitive space, where the students are enthusiastic to gain more attention and knowledge. There will be a questioning of the order and an overthrow of rules to achieve what they desire. There is passion, energy and vulnerability and each student and teacher is an active participant in the pedagogical process rather than a passive recipient and provider of information. Hence, it is imperative to nurture the erotic energy and to tame and keep it under control. A classroom envisioned by Bell Hooks is a far-fetched goal but it is desirable to work towards it along with addressing the problems that arise with it. The first step towards it is to acknowledge the presence of bodies and hence, eros, rather than striving to eliminate it. Research can be furthered by exploring the nature of inequalities that are based on sociocultural prejudices, hierarchies and disabilities that challenge inclusivity rather than just physical appearance, attraction and desire.

References

- Burch, Kerry. "Eros as the Educational Principle of Democracy". Studies in Philosophy and Education, Kluwer Academic Publishers, 1999, pp. 123-142, //doi.org/10.1023/ A:1005136031008
- Fraser, Cameron and Davida Garvin. "Erotic Pedagogy: A Student's and Professor's Perspectives", //docplayer.net/ 45151280-Erotic-pedagogy-a-student-s-and-professor-s-

perspectives.html Hooks, Bell. "Ecstasy". Teaching to Transgress, Routledge, 1994, pp. 201-208 Hooks, Bell. "Eros, Eroticism, and the Pedagogical Process". Cultural Studies, Edited by Henry A. Girroux and Peter McLaren, Vol. 7, No. 1, 1993, pp. 59-64, //cachescan.bcub.ro/13-07-2016P/558258.pdf#page=66

- Hooks, Bell. "Passionate Pedagogy; Erotic Student/Faculty Relationships." Z Magazine, 1996, pp. 45-51.
- Kazan, Tina S. "Dancing Bodies in the Classroom: Moving toward an Embodied Pedagogy". Pedagogy, Vol. 5, No. 3, 2005, pp. 379-408, Project Muse, //muse.jhu.edu/article/187473/pdf?casa_token=FcVTL0mRRYYAAAAA:AvuZx0sdZc1202 S-q77pl4OdHScCLBN60HJxp6ozuj OcdVEVxxxPEAnW3hooJK3Jh12I6Y2sOLw
- Kenklies, Karsten. "The Struggle to Love: Pedagogical Eros and the Gift of Transformation". Journal of Philosophy of Education, Vol. 53, No. 3, 2019, pp. 547-559.
- Leggo, Carl. "Dancing with Desire: A Meditation on Psychoanalysis, Politics, and Pedagogy". Teachers and Teaching: theory and practice, Vol. 2, No. 2, 1996, pp. 233-242, DOI: 10.1080/1354060960020205
- Shapiro, Lawrence and Shannon Spaulding. "Embodied Cognition". The Stanford Encyclopedia of Philosophy (Winter 2021 Edition), Edward N. Zalta (ed.), 21 Sep. 2021, //plato.stanford.edu/archives/win2021/entries/embodied-cognition/> Accessed 25 Dec. 2022
- Pryer, Alison. "'What Spring Does With the Cherry Trees': The Eros of Teaching and Learning". Teachers and Teaching, Vol. 7, No. 1, 2010, pp. 75-88, //doi.org/10.1080/713698758 Schroeder, Celeste Snowber. A Poetics of Embodiment: cultivating An Erotics of the Everyday. 1998, Simon Fraser University, PhD Dissertation. //www.nlc-bnc.ca/obj/s4/f2/dsk2/ftp02/NQ37752.pdf?is_thesis=1&oclc_number=473649 36

Arunima A. V., is currently a research scholar in the department of English Literature at English and Foreign Languages University, Hyderabad. She completed her Master's degree in 2022, from Jawaharlal Nehru University, New Delhi. She is working on the memoirs of people with schizophrenia, looking at them through the lens of cognitive science, psychology, and narratology. Her wide interests are life writings, poetry, cognitive literary studies, and medical humanities.

• • •

Construing Representation of Queer Characters in Indian Cinema

Bashisha Lizza L. Rani[1] and Dr. Ehboklang Pyngrop[2]

1 5th Semester English Honors, Department of English, Synod College, Shillong

2 Assistant Professor, Department of English, Synod College, Shillong

Abstract

With the advent of the repeal of 377, the taboo believed of the LGBTQA+ community has been rapidly losing into a more accepted sphere. The 21st century does not portray a much-anticipated modern thought in India, the reason being people are still skeptical towards the community due to various reasons like religion, societal pressure, and traditional practices. Movies are supposedly the reflection of society. It embeds in itself the very essence of society and its formation. The LGBTQA+ representation in Indian movies is limited to very minute roles. They are usually ridiculed or presented in a humorous aspect. This paper titled 'Construing Representation of Queer Characters in Indian Cinema' will attempt to explore the narratives given to the characters in select Indian movies that represents the LGBTQA+ community. As mentioned before the roles assigned to characters representing the community is seen often as a comic relief, for example, Kal Ho Na Ho. In these select movies, the characters are presented in a feminine or masculine traits since it is misunderstood that gay men always feel the need to cross-dress or act feminine whereas lesbians are tomboys. The issue of gender trouble is being analyzed throughout films, where there is a lot of disruption of accepted notions of homosexuality through the LGBTQ+ people of the films. Hence, the paper will explore the roles played by the LGBTQ+ characters and their representation in the movies.

Keywords: Gender, Cinema, LGBTQA+, Representation

Introduction

Cinema is the art of creating movies and "Movies happen to be the most influential tool of communication" (Abbas & Zohra 35). India is well known for having one of the world's largest film industries, where "about 800 to 1000 movies are made in India every year, which is more than double the number of films Hollywood makes each year" (Sridhar and Mattoo, 4) and its commercial cinema is the most popular form of cinema in India which is commonly known as Bollywood. In India, cinema is a powerful medium which can portray both art forms and social reality and "society happens to learn a lot of things from films" (Ghosal, 507). The queer community in this country—which includes those who identify as LGBTQA+, has benefited from the influence of cinema. Hindi films featuring queer narratives presume that the LGBTQ characters will exhibit hyper-masculinity, which will be made obvious and will heighten the queer gaze. The amplification of male stereotyped behavior is typically more prevalent in queer films from the past. The Supreme Court's judgment on the 6th September, 2018 that the Indian Penal Code (IPC), Section 377 removal, saying that it violated the constitutional right to equality and dignity in hopes to change the country's perception on the LGBT community. The Indian Cinema's projection on the LGBTQIA+ are based on stereotypes which leads to the misrepresentation of gender roles, which leaves a bad impression on the human's mind generation after generation and "clips of alternative sexuality were used to make the audience laugh which was found illogical most of the time." (Gopinath, 2000)

Homosexuality has been a controversial issue in India for many years. Until recently, homosexual acts were considered illegal under Section 377 of the Indian Penal Code, which forbad any such sexual activities against the order of nature. The law had a significant impact on the LGBTQ+ community in India, as it led to widespread discrimination, harassment, and abuse.

Section 377 was overturned by the Supreme Court of India in September 2018 and decriminalized homosexuality. This ruling was celebrated by the LGBTQ+ community and its allies as it is a significant step forward for human rights and equality in India. However, discrimination and stigma against LGBTQ+ individuals continue to be a significant problem in many parts of the country, and LGBTQ+ people still face many challenges in exercising their rights and accessing basic services.

Despite these challenges, there is a growing movement for LGBTQ+ rights in India, and many activists and organizations are working to raise awareness and promote acceptance and equality for all. Several western nations, most recently the U.S., have made marriage equality legal. The newly instated constitution of Nepal, India's neighbor in the north, expressly states "protection, empowerment or advancement of gender-based and sexually orientated minorities," aside from the fact that the UK no longer possesses such a clause. India, being the biggest democracy in the world is having trouble developing economically because of Section 377. Section 377 maintained and produced a new class of citizens who are viewed as untouchables because to their sexual preference and gender. Although in Hinduism there are gender fluid deities, in the Mahabharata features a transgender character named Sikhandin. In the Bible it has only mentioned that God has made a man and woman to populate the earth as recorded in Genesis and gospeler Mathew's record on the parable of the healthy tree, it is just a way to tell the Israelites to reproduce and expand their kingdom in those days.

In movies they are portrayed as grotesque and flamboyant characters who exist only for comic relief or as perverse villains. Indian movies gave the LGBT community quite a bad name, which results in the people from the community unable to come out and remain closeted after being criminalized, hesitated, condemn, and shunned from the majority. The films analyzed the problem of gender inequality, and many of the LGBTQ characters in the movies challenge conventional ideas about homosexuality. Indian cinema has the capacity and the capability to mould the attitude of the Indians and create an awareness among the majority of the population so that society will learn how to understand and have a sense of acceptance towards the community. However, Indian cinema could not break the taboo and still treat queer characters as an element for humor.

The limitations of conventional LGBT (lesbian, gay, bisexual, and transgender) theory led to the emergence of an interdisciplinary area of research known as queer theory in the course of the 1980s and 1990s through various studies and activism. The term 'queer' is used as a way of rejecting the idea that sexuality and gender are fixed and binary, and instead sees them as fluid and constantly in flux.

Indian Cinema and Sexuality

In the commencement of representation, movies did not go into depth about the subject of homosexuality, and the portrayal, to the extent that it was done, had an unintended harmful effect on the audience and society as a whole. However, this topic gained popularity after Deepa Mehta's film Fire. The way that sexual minorities are portrayed in movies today has a remarkable influence on society. Furthermore, despite the fact that some films portray the clan as accepting, there are still several that have anti-clan themes. The movie Fire is one of the most beautiful visual representations of two women in love. Bollywood gave enough representation to the lesbian troupe in the film industry but it did nothing to help with the obvious stereotypes. In the movie Khatra: Dangerous (2022), over-sexualizes gay women and portrays them as the antagonists who turned into psychopaths because of their sexuality Bose comments that "it's the idea that gay men are a caricature – an abnormal version of an actual human being". Mandi a movie which was way ahead of its time, starring Shabana Azmi and Smita Patil, is one of the most thrilling Lesbian representations and portrays an interesting love story between two in-laws. The movie Ek Ladki Ko Dekha To Aisa Laaga, is a strong representation of the Lesbian community and its tagged prejudices.

Bollywood has a long history of stereotyping gay men by exaggerating and misrepresenting them. It has always been for the poor comic relief and the use of humor to humiliate the gay character which might consist of homophobic comments. The gay man's character is often used as a friend of the female lead, who helps her with fashion or correlated to femininity as also supported by Kaur stating that "In mainstream Hindi movies, there have been very few lesbian, gay or transgender leading characters. The mainstream filmmakers are increasingly happy to have non-heterosexuals in supporting roles-often the 'gay best friend' character" (Kaur 1). The Gay character is always being seen to exhibit feminine personality to the point of receiving homophobic slurs for he does not carry any masculine qualities. Queer theory argues that societal norms and expectations around gender and sexuality have been constructed and imposed, rather than being natural or innate. It critiques the notion of a normal heterosexuality and instead seeks to broaden and deepen our understanding of sexual orientation and gender identity.

Dostana (2008), is a movie about two Cis-het men pretending to be a gay couple just for the sake of renting a house and uses the mother's reactions for petty humor. Priyanka Chopra, Abhishek Bachchan, and John Abraham play faux gay actors in the film. In the movie, there are situations where John Abraham sweeps Abhishek off his feet and kisses him. The movie, however, made a mockery of the gay community by showcasing the two faux characters pretending to be in a relationship just to get a rented place, as well as get close to the heroine, when in reality, gay couples are often dismissed by land or house owners due to their orientation. Another movie which uses the same strategy to show the shock and disgusted reaction from another character is the movie Kal Ho Na Ho, where they use Kanta Bai's reaction towards Saif Ali Khan's character being Gay. This shows how Indian cinema lacks proper gay representation. One of the key goals of queer theory is to challenge the oppressive systems and structures that marginalize and discriminate against those who identify as LGBTQ+. It aims to undermine heteronormativity—the presumption that everyone is heterosexual and that gender adheres to established binary norms—and to dismantle the connections between privilege and sexual orientation and gender identity that underpin power structures.

Kapoor And Sons, by Shakun Batra, gave less importance to the 'perfect son' being a closeted gay, but is more focused on how Indian families would deal with coming out and in the end of the day he is still the same son no matter who he chooses to be with.

Aligarh, (2016) is a beautiful movie about a Professor from Aligarh Muslim University, how his sexuality made him lose his occupation. He then meets a journalist which later helps him. It is biographical in nature, a drama film that was written and directed by Hansal Mehta. The movie is based on an actual account of Aligarh Muslim University Marathi professor 'Dr. Shrinivas Ramchandra Siras', who was fired due to his sexual orientation. In his observations about the movie, Rao states that,

A few scenes in Hansal Mehta's quiet, reflective film persuade us that we are capable of looking at the subject with understanding, compassion and sensitivity. With anger that has purpose and sees the inhumanity and injustice of what happened to Dr. Siras but without being self-righteous — normally the bane of films with a cause. (Rao, 1)

Compared to the other sexuality, Bisexuality is the least explored topic, Bisexual individuals often gets stigmatized and discriminated. Indian cinema has done not much to change people's opinion about bisexuality.

Margarita With A Straw by Shonali Bose, is the only movie that has actually given bisexuals a proper representation. It is an interesting story about Laila's self-journey with her cerebral palsy and exploring her sexuality. Laila and Khanum from Margarita With A straw, in which one is seen moving around in a wheelchair and another girl who is visually handicapped is given typical clothing, mannerisms, and attire. Similar to earlier films, there is no machismo among LGBT characters, and the movie's lesbian representations don't suffer from showgirl mentality. The movie Dedh Ishqiya, starring Madhuri and Huma who are projected as heterosexual women, they are often seen getting intimate with each other, yet it did not have the potential to deliver a clear and powerful message about Bisexuality. Honeymoon Travels PVT Limited, is a movie about a married couple, but the wife somehow found out that her husband is bisexual, even though in the movie the word 'bisexuality' was never used.

Indian cinema has always misrepresented the Trans community by giving Trans role to cis actors, and the ideal role of a Trans character is either the villain hijra or a cross-dresser used for a comic relief. Transgender people have endured a great deal of suffering as a result of historically inaccurate depictions that depict them as predatory and sexually deviant (Sangharsh), evil (Maharani in Sadak), or treated as minor characters who are either mercilessly killed off to serve poor writing or used as comic relief throughout the film (Masti, Laxmii). These representations "other" individuals who already identify with sexually minority groups, and any humor gained from putting down these communities, it is clear, exists purely the cis-het sexual objectification. Bhugra, Kalra, & Ventriglio suggest that,

These films portrayed and used third gender stereotypes mostly for comic relief and ended up validating those stereotypes. Any person who identified themselves with the LGBTQIA+ community was viewed as someone from the sexual minority because having a sexual identity other than the dominant one is still, to a great extent considered as 'unnatural' and a 'western import' in our country.

(Bhugra, et al, 5)

Movies such as Raja Hindustani (1996) is a perfect example to this, not only that the movie misguides the characters' gender but also shows the protagonist as a sexist. The movie is filled with scenes that portray misogyny. The characters Kamal Singh and Balwant Singh whose genders and sexuality are difficult to identify gets poked fun by one of the cis-het male characters from the movie only for comedy effect without proper knowledge of their 'actual' gender. Another movie called Tammana, it is a movie directed by Mahesh Bhatt which concerns and builds the stereotypical representation of the hijra's identity.

Another movie named Sadak, where Maharani's character is the evil transgender pimp who runs a brothel, which leaves a negative representation of the transgender community. Director Mahesh Bhatt cast Sadashiv Amrapurkar as 'Maharani,' a villainous lady who functioned as the film Sadak's major antagonist, a first of its kind in Hindi cinematic history. Although the actor won a Filmfare Award for his performance, the part did little to alter how society viewed eunuchs. In the movie, she was presented as a disgusting brothel owner who exploited and mistreated young girls. In a film where the transgender character had so much screen time, the falsehoods about the transgender community were frequently repeated, which ultimately resulted in the creation of a stereotype in Indian popular culture.

Numerous disciplines, including literature, sociology, psychology, cultural studies, and political science, among others, have been significantly impacted by queer theory. The ongoing LGBTQ+ rights movement has also benefited from its influence, and it has served as motivation for activism and advocacy efforts to advance equality and fairness for every individual, irrespective of gender identity or sexuality.

Conclusion

The LGBTQIA+ representation in the Indian cinema is still based on stereotypes but they are taking baby steps towards understanding what the community actually is. Due to the widespread prejudice against gays in our society, these films faced a great deal of public backlash, which led to a fall in the number of daring films challenging the social taboo Although one cannot express that these movies would have been better if the queer character roles are given to an actual person from the community, still things would have been less awkward and stereotypical than giving roles that represent the LGBTQIA+ community to a cis-heterosexual person. Even if these movies shed some light on the people, it still has a long way to go for Bollywood to declare that they are giving a proper representation to the people of the community.

The portrayal of gay characters and themes in Indian movies has been a sensitive issue in recent years. While homosexuality was decriminalized in India in 2018, it still remains a taboo subject in many parts of the country and is not widely accepted in the mainstream.

It is important to note that representation in popular media, including movies, can have a significant impact on shaping public attitudes and opinions. So, while there is still a long way to go in terms of wider acceptance and inclusion of the LGBTQ+ community in India, the increasing visibility in popular culture will certainly be a step in the right direction.

References

- Abbas, H. Q., & Zohra, F. T. "Construction of differences through movies: A case study of portrayal of Kashmiri Muslims in Indian movies". Cross-Cultural Communication, 9(6). 2013. 35–39.
- Bhugra, Dinesh et al. "Portrayal of Gay characters in Bollywood cinema." International review of Psychiatry. Abingdon, England. Vol. 27. 2015.
- Bose, S. "Popular Indian Cinema's Complicated Relationship With LGBTQIA+ Representation". Elle. 2022. https://elle.in/lgbtqia-representation-in-popular-indian-cinema-2/
- Ghosal, A. "Impact of Indian sports movies on sports culture of India". International Journal of Physiology, Nutrition and

Physical Education, Vol. 3(2), 2018. 507–511.

- Gopinath, G. "Queering Bollywood: alternative sexualities in popular Indian cinema." Journal of homosexuality vol. 39,3-4. 2000: 283-97.
- Kaur, P. "Queer Hindi Cinema: A Study on Understanding LGBT Identities". International Journal For Innovative Research In Multidisciplinary Field. Volume - 3, Issue - 3. 2017
- Luther J. Daniel. "The Karan Johar playbook: The open secret, male same-sex sexuality, and the 'big-brand' in Bollywood". South Asian Popular Culture. Vol. 19. 2021.
- Rao, M. "Exploring the Theme of Homosexuality in Indian Cinema". Man's World India. 2016. https://www.mansworldindia.com/more/news/exploring-homosexuality-indian-cinema-films/
- Sridhar, S.N. and Mattoo, N.K. "Ananya, A Portrait of India". Associations of Indians in America. New York. 1997
- Srinivas, S.V. "Gandhian Nationalism and Melodrama in the 30's Telugu Cinema". Journal of Moving Image. 1999.
- Singh, I. Gender relations and cultural ideology in Indian cinema. Deep and Deep Publications. New Delhi, India. 2007.

---

[1]Bashisha Lizza L. Rani is a twenty-year-old college student, 6 th semester, English Honours, Synod College, Shillong, Meghalaya, a poet and an artist. She is deeply inspired by the works of Osamu Dazai, Franz Kafka and Edgar Allen Poe.

[2]Dr. Ehboklang Pyngrope is an Assistant Professor in the Dept. of English, Synod College. He has published several papers in UGC CARE and Peered review journals, as well as two books, collection of poems, one titled 'Asylum-Innervation of the Soul' and the other titled; 'Of Gardens and Flowers'.

• • •

CHAPTER V

Inclusion of Third Gender: An Analytical Reading of Select Bollywood Films

Bhavya Pahuja

Ph.D. Research Scholar, Centre for Comparative Literature & Translation Studies, Central University of Gujarat, Gandhinagar, Sector 29, Gujarat

Abstract

The present eruption of talks on gender minorities has led to their cinematic representation at national and international levels. The term transgender gets embedded with LGBTQ group which dissociates itself from both male or female gender and is generally referred as 'third gender'. This paper is a study of the explicit portrayal of trans community in Bollywood films which is either disregarded or has controversial consequences. There are a range of films right from *Darmiyaan*(1997) to the recent *Chandigarh Kare Aashiqui*(2021), which did not show up positive and overwhelming response from the audience. Such kind of films become the subject in this research where the transgenders are presented as eminent characters. Although their inclusion can be seen as a mark of modernism where representation from every stratum has become necessary yet this inclusion is always taken up in a demeaning manner. This study aims at looking the paradigmatic shift (if there is) of the portrayal of transgenders from the early times to that of contemporary period. It also analyses the stereotypes and stigma associated with the third gender roles. The methodology employed in the research is of content analysis with queer and film theory working simultaneously.

Keywords: transgender, inclusivity, Bollywood movies, third gender, discourse

---

Introduction

Postmodern art forms characteristically stay in opposition to the mainstream culture with multiplicity, genre mixing and a rebellious sort of temperament and cinema is the most popular cultural form which provide a clear-cut articulation of contemporary thoughts and discourses which largely include the marginal and controversial discourses. The earlier dominant themes of patriarchy were replaced or experimented with the coming of feminist approach in 1970s, producers and audience both started to look for other neglected themes like race, class, ethnicity, sexuality, etc. the subject of multiple sexual identities now came into question which embodied gays, lesbians, bisexuals, transgenders and encompassing all were queer. This sexual identification was largely ignited by Judith Butler's assertion that gender is a social construct than being a natural phenomenon. It's the continuous performance of gender (male/female) that leads to a general understanding and differentiating in the society over gender. Butler's analysis paved way for the inclusion and development of queer theory which is an exploration of sexual identity. In her work *Bodies That Matter: On the Discursive Limits of Sex,* she defines a queer as "a discursive rallying point for younger lesbians and gays(...)and for bisexuals and straights for whom the term expresses an affiliation with anti-homophobic politic." (Butler)

Nayar simply points out Queer studies as "an attempt to redefine identities and carve out a cultural/political space within the dominant heterosexual paradigm, to simply stop being invisible or the "perverted" or "sick" "other" of heterosexuality." (Nayar)

Transgenders are those who do associate themselves with the sex they were assigned at the time of birth. They are referred as 'third' or 'other' gender. The term encompasses transman, transwoman, cross-dressed, transsexual, transvestites. They are called as *hijra* and *kinnar* in India. These people may or may not go through some medical treatment to match their physical body with their sexual identity. Here, in Indian cultural construction, their blessings are sought in marriages, to a new born child yet they are considered as outsiders in the society. Their customs, rituals and traditions are different, separated from the rest of 'heterosexual society' and means of earning are singing, dancing, donations from their performances and even begging. Because of their nonconformity to the society standards or characteristics they have been marginalised, discriminated, suppressed and ill-treated. At every stage, they have to make people understand their gendered identity and how it is different from their biological sexual identity. This understanding becomes problematic 'because trans people do not fit into the traditional neat categories of male or female.' (Doughty and Etherington-Wright)

Since ages, the reins of power have been pulled mainly by the males and these feminists' protests against male oriented society have somehow brought them into light. But the struggle of transgenders, although gave constitutional recognition to them yet it seems, will remain an everlasting one in terms of public respect. Recently in 2019, a bill was introduced in India stating the protection of transgenders. Yes, this inclusion is noteworthy but still they have not got the social acceptance and a sense of security as their parents are also ashamed of giving birth to a 'non-binary'. For people, a healthy and normal society comprises reproduction which the transgenders are not capable of, that is why this impotence make them to be labelled as defective, adulterated or abnormal. This male/female binary setup keeps the third sex at bay ignoring their concerns, rights and issues. Because of this negligence, they have to live a life of stigma and stain, governed be the major chunk of society i.e., heterosexuals. So, in reality they are denied basic rights like education, healthcare, employment (other than their 'stereotypical' jobs) and marry with their choice. Michael Foucault in his work *The Order of Discourse* has the best explanation for these 'excluded' outsiders who remain in the periphery of 'discourse':

Rather than seeing discourse as simply a set of statements which have some coherence, we should, rather, think of a discourse as existing because of a complex set of practices which try to keep them in circulation and other practices which try to fence them off from others and keep those other statements out of circulation.

Bollywood and Transgenders

Bollywood films are widely circulated not just in the country only but also worldwide. When we look at these films, after the independence, their prominent depiction is of male-female relationships and some villain in it. Exploring gender related themes began only in the late twentieth century and even in such films, most of them were female oriented and just indifferent towards the lives of third gender. The 'power structure' (as Foucault calls it) manifests itself through such institutions like cinema where projection of patriarchal hierarchy and subjugation of other gender is used as a tool.

With the coming of globalization, cinema started to incorporate people from every stratum of the society to match up the level of western nations. So 21st century marks the imbibing of gays, lesbians, transexuals in Indian art forms. But In cinema particularly such characters are either portrayed in comic role or as criminals, hardly their actual lives, struggles are depicted there. The heterosexual 'hegemony' (as Gramsci calls it) which is responsible for subverting these 'marginal' voices, dominate the Indian culture and cinema. This stereotypical presentation is one of the main reasons why the transgender community is not progressing or why they are not getting the social respect that they deserve. Even in news and media also they are shown in negative light and uncapable of doing anything productive for the society.

Neither In nor Out in *Darmiyaan* (In Between)

This film stars Kiran Kher, Arif Zakaria (the intersex) as the lead actors. The film is a bold move on director Kalpana Lajmi's part as there is direct portrayal of transgenders and their issues, use of abusive dialogues, prostitution. Such kind of depiction in that era when talking about transgenders was considered a taboo, is one of its kind as it is one of the earliest films (1997) based on the life of a transgender. The plot revolves around the struggles that *Immi* goes through because of his gender. The protagonist *Immi* is born a transgender to *Zeenat Begum* (Kiran Kher) but his mother does not send him in the eunuchs' community and does not pay heed to their warnings. His friends tease him for not having the penis same as rest of the boys. His mother is not even ready to accept that she gave birth to a transgender and tells him to call her *aapa* (elder sister) and not *ammi* (mother). His father also left him after knowing his identity but at last he accepts him. The humiliation which every transgender in the country faces is also the same with *Immi*. When he is unable to find a job, he is forced to join the *hijra* community and perform the same acts as the rest do. After he got raped, he criticises everyone in the community for leading such miserable lives. In one scene from the film, we see that they talk in their group about their denial rights, their miseries, their treatment as if they are not human beings:

humein bank mein khata nahi kholne dete
train mein nahi chhadne dete, vote nahi dene dete
mandir se masjid tak khaded dete hain
In English-
they (society) can't let us open bank account
they don't allow us to enter in trains, cast vote
they throw us out of temples and mosques.

Transgenders are not accepted for having (adopting) kids, which we clearly witness in the case of *Immi*. Their love, warmth and compassion for a child is same as any other mother but the society does not let them express their love. What is left for them is to survive all alone in their life. What the film conveys is that peace and liberation to a eunuch is possible only after death which is shown in ending of the film when *Immi* kills himself and his mother and finally calls her *ammi jaan* (mother) and she also addresses him as *mera beta* (my son).

Transcending the conventions in *Shabnam Mousi*

This film (2005) is based on real life transgender named Shabnam Bano who is the first elected transgender MLA in India. Directed by Yogesh Bharadwaj, it stars Ashutosh Rana as the lead actor playing the role of a transgender *Shabnam*. This film reflects the plight of transgenders, what kind of attitude from the society they have to face. They are forced to work as servants, prostitutes, and treated as criminals. Although they are considered as God's pious creation, we see that they have to become sex workers also for sustenance. They wander here and there homelessly and loving or marrying a man is just not possible for them for society does not grant them the permission. There is a conversation between *Shabnam* and her transgender mother *Halima:*

Shabnam's maai: jis samaj se humein sirf tiraskaar mila hai usse puruskar ki ummeed mat kar.

Shabnam: Kyun maai? Kya sirf isliye ki hum hijra hai? Humein janm bhi to isi samaj ne diya hai. Napunsak mard aur baanjh aurat bhi to humare jaise hote hain par samaj ne unka bahishkaar to nahi kiya na.

In English:

Shabnam's transgender mother: do not expect any reward from the society which has given us contempt only.

Shabnam: Why mom? Just because we are eunuchs? We are given birth by this society only. Impotent men and women are also like us but society does not boycott them.

Here we see that most of these eunuchs have complaints against the society but because they are the subject of suppression under the hands of 'heterosexuals', they don't raise their voice against anyone. They desire to get education, become teachers, farmers, artists like any other human but society's biased perspective that they need to sustain on others' alms, become the hindrance for them. The audience witness the battle which *Shabnam* fights tobecome a politician- she is not even allowed to enter the public office, there is no mention of the third gender category in the nomination form. *Shabnam's* lover's sister *Nazma* warns her by

46

saying

Aapko duniya ke liye hi paida kiya gaya hai, duniyadaari ke liye nahi. Jab khuda ne aapko aurat ya mard ka naam nahi diya to aap jo hain wahi bane rahiye- aadhi adhoori.

In English-

You are born for this world not for worldliness. When God did not give you the name of a man or a woman, so be the same as you are- split and incomplete.

The opposition leader feels shameful fighting the election against a transgender and thinks that even his win would be a defeat for the opponent is a transgender. *Shabnam*'s character comes out as a bold and powerful one as she is able to change the heart of the man who was supposed to murder her. Not just this, she wins the election by winning the hearts of all the villagers and her honesty. The film is quite successful in the projection of a powerful transgender role. It manages to deviate from the conventional and stereotypical role assigned to a transgender.

A not so substantial theme in *Laxmii*

Laxmii, a film directed by Raghav Lawrence, released in 2020 on OTT platform depicts very less regarding transgenders' experiences as compared to the other films studied in this work. This horror comedy, starrer Akshay Kumar, Sharad Kelkar is showing a very passive role of the eunuch *Laxmi*. The plot gets unravelled after the hero Asif gets possessed by the ghost of *Laxmi* who tells her story while she was alive. In a very short part of the film, we get to know of the atrocities done on her, and her fellow transgender Geeta. Its only in the latter half of the show that the audience gets to know of *Laxmi's* story, her struggles and her disrupted childhood. Bereft of the basic rights like education, she was thrown out of the house and left like an orphan by her own parents. Although we see that to what heights these people can reach if given a chance, given education. In Laxmi's speech, she laments of being in the state of a trans by saying

Maine kya nasha kiya, juaa khela, murder kiya kisi ka jo itni badi saza di mujhe, arey wo to bhagwan ne humein aisa banaya, meri kya galti hai isme

In English-

Did I use alcohol or gambled or murdered someone that I got such a huge punishment. It was God who created me like this, where am I at fault?

She urges the listeners not to treat their eunuch child the same way as was she treated, also to give her education in life. *Laxmi* and her caretaker were killed for the land *Laxmi* had brought for her community's welfare. The theme pertaining to transgenders is more or less eclipsed under the horror comic scenes in the film. The ending shows their ritual of worshipping god *Shiva* on a full moon night and the revenge *Laxmi* takes by killing her murderers.

Modernized transsexual in *Chandigarh Kare Aashiqui*

Released in 2021, this film is an example of the recent trends in Hindi cinema which now makes room for the earlier marginalised themes. Directed by Abhishek Kapoor the film is about the social acceptance which trans people don't get in the Indian society. The lead actress Vaani Kapoor (Maanvi) here plays the role of a trans girl. She was born a boy but later got her sex changed after surgery. The hero Manvinder (Ayushman Khurana) likes her in the beginning but as soon as he gets to know that she is a trans girl, he is ashamed of hooking up with a boy. Forget the rest of people, Maanvi's own mother is not ready to accept the fact that she gave birth to a trans girl. She calls her Manu, not Maanvi and even breaks her relation with Maanvi for she changed her gender. Maanvi develops feminine traits like dressing up like women, wearing long hair, getting facial treatments for skin upliftment After Maanvi's revelation of being a trans girl she has to face insult by everyone in the society and is called by various names like *chhakka* and *kinnar.* She is not invited in the family functions because of her sexual orientation, and treated like an outcast. In a shot, Maanvi simply puts out the mindset of the society regarding transgenders by saying to her father

Humesha main kyun chhod ke jau? school chhodo, colony chhodo, Ambala chhodo, gym chhodo...main jo hun wo hun. I am not ashamed

of it.

In English

Why should I leave everytime? I left school, colony, Ambala and now gym...I am what I am and I am not ashamed of it.

Manvinder then tries to learn about the process of that transformation which a transexual goes through. In the final section of the film, we see that the hero goes against his family and society at large by proposing the same trans girl whom he rebuffed earlier. This act may be seen as a blow to the conventional societal norms related to gender. This film falls into a category where the stereotypical roles affixed to the third gender are played with and a modernised version is displayed which enables the audience to view the discourse empathetically.

Conclusion

Cinema can be the powerful medium to generate awareness regarding the injustices towards third gender instead of just portraying their stereotypical roles. Just the inclusion of these people in cinema or literature is not sufficient, what is needed is powerful and strong representation and the real consciousness of transgenders. There are various perspectives on transgenders that need to worked upon by including real life transgenders in pictures. The above-mentioned films show the lacunae still present in the Hindi films regarding the context of third gender.

References

- Benyahia, Casey Sarah, and Claire Mortimer. *Doing Film Studies: A Subject Guide for Students (Doing... Series).* 1st ed., Routledge, 2012.
- Butler, Judith. *Bodies That Matter: On the Discursive Limits of Sex.* 1st ed., Routledge, 2011.
- Doughty, Ruth, and Christine Etherington-Wright. *Understanding Film Theory.* Zaltbommel, Netherlands, Van Haren Publishing, 2017.
- *Selections From the Prison Notebooks.* International Publishers, 1971.

- Subhan, Habib. "Tryst With Destiny: Sexual Discourse and Third Gender in Select Indian Bollywood Films." *International Journal of Humanities and Social Science Invention*, Aug. 2013, 34-42.
- Young, Robert Ed. *Untying the Text*. First Printing, Routledge Kegan and Paul, 1982.
- **Films Cited:**
- Audiolab Music. "Shabnam Mausi Full Movie Hindi | Real Life Story | Ashutosh Rana | Sabnam Moshi." *YouTube*, 1 May 2020, www.youtube.com/watch?v=dtbNL35wPdg.
- "Chandigarh Kare Aashiqui." *Netflix*, 2021, www.netflix.com/in/title/81323993?source=35.
- *Laxmii.* 2020, www.hotstar.com/in/movies/laxmii/1260036200/watch?utm_source=gwa.
- Soham Rockstar Entertainment. "Darmiyaan - in Between |Hindi Movie |Kiron Kher,Arif Zakaria, Tabu, Shahbaaz Khan,Sayaji S#Darmiyaan." *YouTube*, 21 July 2022, www.youtube.com/watch?v=7NwxKELYguU.

Bhavya Pahuja, is a Ph.D. Research Scholar in the Centre for Comparative Literature & Translation Studies, Central University of Gujarat, Gandhinagar. She completed her bachelor's and master's degree in English Literature from Maharaja Ganga Singh University, Bikaner, Rajasthan. She is currently working under Prof. Balaji Ranganathan on South Asian cinema in Central University of Gujarat.

• • •

CHAPTER VI

Inclusivity of the Marginalised People of Kerala in the 19th Century: with Special Reference to the Role of Christian Missionaries

C. J. Ginsen

Ph.D. Scholar in History, PSMO College Tirurangadi, University of Calicut, Malappuram, Kerala

Abstract

Christian missionaries has built a just society where no one is rejected or relegated to the margins of society is immense. As the members of the religious congregation, they initially founded followed the same path, long-term changes took place. Although the services and historical contexts they have initiated are small and limited, they are worth mentioning in the mainstream. They have tried to uplift the marginalized group mostly through educational policies. They were able to change many social environments that existed in Kerala in the nineteenth century.

Introduction

Many changes occurred in 19th-century Kerala as well. Inequalities in the caste system were one of the most serious issues they faced. The impact of colonization resulted in some educational changes. The encounter with Christian missionaries was one of the most important events in Kerala's history. During this time, LMS (London Mission Service) and CMS (Church Mission Service

Society) missionaries came to Travancore and creatively engaged in concretizing the lower castes' human rights. In 1817, the CMS missionaries established the first college in Kottayam, where students from all castes were admitted, breaking the higher castes' monopoly on the exclusive privilege of higher education. The Basel mission was working in Malabar where the caste structure was less strong and was more liberal in admitting students from lower castes to their educational institutions.1

Rather than simply doing missionary work, St Chavara was a catholic religious priest who pioneered new ways to make a significant impact in society, such as public education movements, women empowerment strategies, and so on. He established his educational vision, which is still bearing fruit after many decades. In the 19th century scenario, Syrian Catholics also had the privilege of upper caste people2. Arch Deacon Koshi's first Malayalam novel-P 19th century mentioned what kinds of privileges they had at the time. It is critical to recognize the significance of a Syrian priest who worked for the betterment of society by eradicating social inequalities.

Kerala Society In The Early 19th Century

Kerala was enslaved by the caste system in the eighteenth and nineteenth centuries. The deep chasm that separated the high castes from the lower castes concretized thinking along caste lines, and creed was very much the norm. Each caste considered itself superior and kept a safe distance from the others. Despite the concentration of power in the hands of the kings of Travancore and Cochin, and the assumption of direct administration by the English East India Company in Malabar, the upper castes such as the Brahmins, Kshatriyas, and Nairs continued to enjoy several privileges and immunities. Economically, these high castes were the largest landowners, and occupation was also determined by caste. Socially, the caste held its sway. Many people lacked access to education. Inter-dining or intermingling was not permitted. The evil and customs of untouchability, as well as unapproa19[th]-century-see ability, played havoc in those days, and lower castes were not allowed to walk in public places. Keralans were very much bound by the rules and customs of anxiety at the time. It was a patriarchal society, and women had no freedom at home, in society, or the church. Early marriage, lack of rights to family property, and evils in social customs such as the caste system, Marumakkathayam, devadasi system, and Sambandham made women's lives miserable.

The situation of the lower castes was not much better. They were denied social freedom, education, and property rights, and they lived on landlords' land and worked as bonded laborers for them. Human dignity was at a crossroads, and her refusal earned her the moniker "lunatic asylum." The role of Chavara Kuriakose Elias in the social reform movement must be remembered against this backdrop. He was a great revolutionary who came before his time, and he was a luminary among India's topmost social reformers. He can be considered the morning star of social reformers.

Reform And The Dalit Rights Movement

The ruling British Raj attempted to abolish some aspects of India's caste system, particularly those about the Untouchables. British liberals saw the treatment of the Untouchables as particularly cruel, possibly due to their lack of faith in reincarnation. Indian reformers joined the cause as well. Jyotiba Phule coined the term "Dalit" to describe and sympathize with the Untouchables. During India's struggle for independence, activists such as Sus Mohan and Das Gandhi championed the cause of the Dalits. To emphasize their humanity, Gandhi dubbed them "Harijan," which means "children of God." Following India's independence in 1947, the new constitution designated groups of former Untouchables as "scheduled castes," earmarking them for special consideration and government assistance. As with the Meiji Japanese designation of former Hinin and Eta outcasts as "new commoners," this emphasized the distinction rather than formally assimilating the traditionally downtrodden groups into society. Eighty years after the term was coined, the Dalits have become a powerful political force in India and enjoy greater access to education. Some Hindu temples allow Dalits to serve as priests. Although they still face discrimination from some quarters, the Dalits are untouchable no longer.

Missionaries Encounter With The Caste Issue In Kerala

During the nineteenth century, when the other Protestant missionaries began their work in Travancore, social relationships were marked by caste distinction, discrimination, and segregation. The missionaries introduced a western concept of equality, as well as the gospel of brotherhood and love, to this society ruled primarily by caste. Despite this, the influence of caste remained in society and within the Church, though the rigidity of caste rules and untouchability began to disappear.3 Many Protestant missionaries who worked in India, particularly in Travancore, taught the people about the evils of caste discrimination. They made special efforts to persuade the people that it was against God's word and that the Christian Church should not accept it in any way. However, among the missionaries, particularly those working in Travancore, there was a strong discriminatory attitude that was as bad as the caste system itself. This is supported by the following incident from the middle of the nineteenth century.

Contributions Of Chavara To Education

Chavara recognized that all forms of discrimination are the result of ignorance, and thus they must be eradicated. Recognizing that education is the only way to eradicate ignorance, he abandoned the idea of instilling literacy in our people. He yearned for social equality and social dignity in a society where people were divided into castes. He was a firm believer in the power of education to bring about social change, mobility, and development. Here we can see Chavara's vision, a great vision of seeing everything as a reflection of God. He saw in each human being, the God himself. So, his vision of education was of an egalitarian nature education for all, irrespective of caste, creed, religion, sex, or anything else. He aimed to achieve this social development through multi-faceted tasks-establishing schools, printing books, emanating the role of a teacher and innovator, and equally through charitable activities. His educational idea was all- inclusive with a secular character.

Women's empowerment programs are a common occurrence in today's society. APJ Abdul Kalam, as quoted in Satru-sally, Women's empowerment is a prerequisite for building a good nation. When women are empowered, a stable society is assured. Women's empowerment is critical because their thoughts and value systems lead to the development of a good family, a good society, and, ultimately, a good nation. The current generation understands that without women's education, sustainable societal growth is impossible. So, the government of India as well as state governments take some admirable steps to ensure the education of women. Even now in this women empowerment era, many interior villages of different Indian states find educating female children meaningless. The gap in male and female literacy rates is higher in some of the states of India; the table establishes this fact.4

He considered education as the central factor for any basic development. Chavara acted as a catalyst for social change, not only to his community but his vision is evident in his interventions in the field of women and the downtrodden too. He understood the fact that the dignity and culture of a society can be detected from the status of women in that society. Empowerment of women leads to benefit not only to the individual woman and women groups but also to the families and community as a whole through collective action for development. Chavara played an important role in diminishing the caste consciousness among the people of Kerala, through the admission of children even from lower classes and castes, in those days of severe caste restrictions. He initiated the task of assimilating the so-called untouchables into mainstream society. With the spread of education, untouchability, unapproachability and other accompanying evils of a caste-ridden society faded into insignificance. The starting of boarding houses, hostels, and orphanages in the centers of the CMI Congregation was a means to uplift the marginalized and economically weaker sections of society. This helped them to come out of their traditional barriers and became capable enough to play their roles in the revolutionary paradigm shift in the socio-cultural development of Kerala. His initiatives are continuing through his Congregations and also through the educationalists of then and now.

A School For Pulaya Converts At Mannanam

Then there's the issue of the ecclesiastical authorities' order to establish a school attached to every church. What kind of school did the order envision? Who gave this order? According to the Mannanam Chronicle, the monastery had received an order from the archbishop to that effect. Many biographers and historians of the time attribute it to St. Chavara. 7 The following is an excerpt from the Mannanam Chronicle: "When Fr. Prior was here (at Mannanam), we received a decree from the archbishop requiring the establishment of a school for the education of boys in every parish." It warned that those who neglected to comply with this order would incur censure. Mannanam Monastery immediately started the construction of a school. We also decided to establish a chapel with a school attached for the pulaya converts". 5The archbishop referred to in the letter is Bernardine Baccinelli who appointed Fr. Chavara as his Vicar general and so the letter might have been originally conceived by St. Chavara and at his request arch bishop willingly promulgated it with the sanction of censure for those who would not comply with the order. The Carmelite tradition was not in agreement with such drastic educational action. As a result, the conclusion that Fr. Chavara was behind this order appears to be very reasonable. The manuscript of the circular is in Chavara's recognized hand and is kept in Mannanam's archives. Though the decree was issued by the Vicar Apostolic, it is most likely that Chavara conceived of the idea and that the decree he prepared was circulated on his recommendation.

Johann Ernst Hanxleden

Johann Ernst Hanxleden, also known as Arnos Paathiri, was a German Jesuit priest. He finished his philosophical studies in Osnabruck before volunteering to serve in India. The perilous journey is described in an account by a doctor, Franz Kaspar Schillinger, who sailed with Arnos Paathri and two other Jesuits, Wilhelm Weber and Wilhelm Meyer. During the voyage, Weber and Meyr died. Arnos arrived in Surat and traveled to Goa. Here he completed his spiritual formation (novitiate) and was sent to Ambazhakkad. Arnos joined the seminary at Sampaloor where he completed his Theological studies. He was ordained priest in 1706.6

Arnos traveled from Goa to Sambalpur in Kochi Kingdom (now Katukutty village panchayat) and received the Vedic title. Because he was at the forefront of language studies, he was sent to Thrissur, the seat of cultural scholars at the time, because of his interest in learning Sanskrit. He became friends with many literary men. However, learning Sanskrit was not easy. Even Shudras were not permitted to learn Sanskrit at the time. The Namburis of the time were not eager to teach Sanskrit to a foreigner who had crossed the sea. But some of the Nambutiris who were productive were close to Pathiri, influenced by his personality, humility, and knowledge. In this way, two Namboothiri's named Kunshan and Krishnan from Angamali became Pathiri's friends. They taught him Sanskrit.7 They gave him Siddharupa written on a palm leaf. He studied epic works like Mahabharata and Ramayana. He learned Sanskrit from his guru, which was a boon to most Europeans. Not only that, he also wrote a grammar book for Sanskrit in a European language. His Namboodiri friends helped him a lot. There are records that he studied with Bishop John Ribeiro of Kodungallur Diocese for four years. It is believed that Arnos Pathiri, who suffered from a stomach-related illness in Puthanchira, moved to Vellore village for treatment.[2] Arnos Pathiri was one of the first Europeans to make a critical study of the tetragrammaton, architecture, astrology, linguistics, and poetry.8

Arnos first came to Pashyangadi in Vellore and started trying to build a small church temporarily there. The King of Kochi initially agreed to give land for it, but later withdrew. But Commander Bernard Ketel, who helped the King of Kochi in the war against the Zamorin, helped Arnos. But this proved to be a source of discomfort with the native Chengazi Nambiar and the King of Kochi. However, Pathiri befriends Arvancheri Tambrakals and Illikal Inayat. It is believed that the Azhvancheri Tambras built the staircase mansion for the Pathiri to live in. The gopuram called Padippuramalika was the first to be built and Arnos Pathiri supervised the construction of the church while staying there. Facing opposition from the king and the local non-Christians, Arnos Pathiri moved to Vengilaseri Ayyappan Hill at Chirama9kad (Sramamkad) near Vellore.

Adappur's greatest contribution to Malayalam literature is his writings on Arnos Pathiri. Adappur, unlike many priests, has always adopted an independent stand and has been bold in his opinions and views whether on religion, literature, culture, or society. And even at this age, he must be nearing 90 years; he has the energy and will to go on with his pursuits. The English word will be another feather in his cap," feels Varghese Angamaly. Arnos Pathiri died of a snake bite in 1732 at Pazhuvil and was buried in the church there. A memorial was built for him outside the church where his mortal remains were kept. A history museum has also come up there9. But in Sampaloor where Paathiris spent his early years and was for long a Jesuit stronghold, whatever remains of the seminary and press need to be cared for.

Ramapuram Kunjachan

Augustine (Ramapuram Kunjachan) was born on 1 April 1891, at Ramapuram in Travancore (present-day Kerala, India). He was the son of Itty Type and Eliswa of the Thevarparambil clan, which is a branch of the Kuzhumbil family lineage. Augustine received his primary education at a school sponsored by the government of Travancore. He advanced to St. Ephrem's School in Mannanam were his religious faith intensified, compelling him to pursue a career as a priest. After completing secondary education at St Ephrem's School, Augustine embarked on a journey on foot from Ramapuram to Changanacherry to enroll in St Thomas Minor Seminary. After receiving his major seminary formation at Puthenpally Seminary in Varapuzha, Augustine was ordained as a priest on July 16, 1915.

After celebrating his first mass at St. Augustine Church in Ramapuram, his home parish, Augustine resided in his home village for eight years while undergoing practical training. He was known as Kunjachan ('little priest' in Malayalam) for his short stature. In 1923, Augustine was appointed as assistant vicar to Thomas Kuzhumpil at St. Sebastian Church in Kadanad. During his vocation in Kadanad, Kunjachan was often approached by the local villagers, who relied on his advice and blessings for their agricultural yield. Kunjachan would sprinkle holy water on crops, ensuring a plentiful harvest. Unfortunately, an illness forced Kunjachan to return to Ramapuram.

Conclusion

Today, Kerala with a prolonged high literacy rate, and high sex ratio is a State with a high Human Development Index and Gender Development Index. This exemplary achievement was not a single day-night activity. Several organizations, governments, and well-wishers put their heads and hands together to achieve this goal. The Christian missionaries have tried the most to bring about such a change. They with their farsightedness firmly believed that a society could make progress only through knowledge and wisdom.

References

- Cf. Fr. Valerian, 1939; K.C. Chacko, 1959; 95; P.T.Thomas, 1956; P.J. Thomas 1961 etc. School in Malayalam is called pallikudam, a hall attached to the church.
- CF. J. Roberts (ed), Caste in its Religious and Civil Character Opposed to Christ, London: Longman, Brown, Green and Longmans, 1847, pp 12-18.
- J.W. Gladstone, "Christian Missionaries and Caste in Kerala", in M.E. Prabhakar (ed), Towards a Dalit Theology, ISPCK, Delhi, 1988, pp.104-105.
- K. Pradeep, The times and life of Arnos Pathiri, the Hindu, KOCHI, AUGUST 07, 2015 17:46 IST
- Koji, Kawashima. Missionaries and a Hindu State. Oxford: Oxford University Press, 1998.

- National Commission on Population, Ministry of Health and Family Welfare, Government of India, http://populationcommission.nic.in/content/933_1_LiteracyRate.aspx, retrieved 22 February 2015.
- Nossiter, Thomas Johnson (1982). "Kerala's identity: unity and diversity". Communism in Kerala: a study in political adaptation. University of California Press. ISBN 978-0- 520-04667-2. Retrieved 9 June 2011.
- Ulakamthara, Mathew (1982). Arnos Pathiri. Kerala History Association. OCLC 17608738.

Fr. Ginsen Chiriyankandath, is a priest of Trichur Archdiocese. He is currently working as the parish priest of St. Joseph's Church Kundukad. He has worked as an Assistant Professor on Govt Contract at St. Thomas College Autonomous Trichur for the last three years. Currently he is pursuing his Doctoral studies at PSMO College Tirurangadi under the University of Calicut.

• • •

CHAPTER VII

A National Inclusive Education Framework to Schools on Their Journey Towards Inclusion

Dr. K. C. Lalithambika

Associate Professor of English & Vice Principal, Thiruthangal Nadar College, Selavayal,Chennai -51, Tamilnadu, India

Abstract

This structure celebrates excellent works that have been done in school for a long time. It attempts to integrate these beneficial methods in order to offer all students, teachers, parents, and the larger community an effective and efficient service. In order to ensure that the educational structure is modified to meet the requirements of the learner and not the additional way around, it is practical sources that invite schools to start a insightful journey to significantly interact with and assess the comprehensive practices in the school community. This framework supports the institution of an comprehensive school atmosphere that ensure that the entire students have the chance to obtain the essential skills and attitude to be energetic citizen and to be successful at effort and in the social order, which is the line with the education strategy of the Ministry for Education and Employment (MEDE) as stated in the structure for the Education policy for Malta 2014–2024 (MEDE, 2014). In the direction of promoting the inclusion of all students community, diversity ought to be recognized in our school and exploited as a teaching prospect.

Keywords: Inclusive Education, Educational System, Efficient and Effective Service, Framework, Education strategy, Teaching Opportunity.

Introduction

The national inclusive education, eliminating inequalities in society and education systems, to examines how the Bangladeshi government has responded to these international pronouncements through a descriptive review of policy papers and reform measures. The review concentrates on problems that help different learners be included in majority primary and secondary schools. The National Education Policy 2010, Bangladesh's most recent strategy, made an effort to improve inclusive education. The subsequent Primary Education Development plan and the education Quality enhancement project, two significant reform projects, both supported inclusiveness. These initiatives to some extent integrated the inclusionary philosophies and practices into the nation's current educational framework. (Ahsan, M. Tariq, and Jahirul Mullick, 2013) Inclusion is becoming more recognized as a key factor in educational reform and as one of the main objectives of the global political agenda. In order to direct their efforts to promote more inclusiveness, a set of schools in one area of Spain tested recently urbanized review mechanism called "Themis," which is described and analyzed in this research. The report then focuses on how schools might be assisted in reviewing their progress toward becoming more inclusive. The difficulty of interpreting reliable evidence, the realities of building stakeholder confidence, the significance of resolve contradiction and tension, and choosing priority for going ahead were some of the difficulties perceived in its application. (Azorín, Cecilia, and Mel Ainscow, 2020),European nations working on "inclusive" educational systems side by side. The national education policy response in Ireland, Austria, Spain, and the Czech nation in modern decades are discussed after a brief outline of the global context for education policy connecting to the education of public with disabilities. This includes both legislation pertaining to extraordinary educational needs and accomplishment of policies in practice. The comparison explores the difficulties that have arisen as different nations attempt to match provisions in existing educational systems with those of international policy, through their own inheritance benefit, pressure, and priority. It things to see the various manifestation of comprehensive education that are currently present in each nation.(Smyth, Fiona, et al.2014)Like many other nations, New Zealand is starting its transition to a more inclusive educational system. New Zealand have the chance to construct addition a reality, but as Skrtic (1991) notes, this require different state of mind built on a diverse knowledge foundation that of conservative extraordinary education paradigms. It is asserted that for this change to take place, exclusionary factors in schools and cultures must be acknowledged, along with the functions they serve.(Kearney, Alison, and Ruth Kane,2006) addition and comprehensive practice; model of unique educational requirements and disability; and the standards that strengthen our thoughts about these matter. Professor Lindsay offers a perceptive assessment of widespread thoughts about inclusion and of present explore methodologies; base his argument on the study findings. Everyone paying attention in the education of children and young community with specific enlightening requirements will find conclusions interesting.(Lindsay, Geoff,2003) social justice and inclusiveness in education. It is one of the few theoretical and political theories that includes disability or destruction in the discussion of social justice and depends on Martha Nussbaum's usage of the capability advance. The following section of the article presents the results of a three-year participatory action research study that involved eight elementary schools in Tanzania's Dares Salaam and Pwani (Coast) areas. The project goal is create a Tanzanian Index of Inclusion. At the governmental, neighborhood, and educational levels, inclusion faces many obstacles. There have been several developments in the direction of inclusive, just, and high-quality education in Tanzania, according to the literature study and the project rising findings, but there is still a long way to go. (Polat, Filiz. 2011) The most significant problem confronting educational systems worldwide is inclusiveness. It offers a structure for identify lever that can aid in reduction system in a more comprehensive way by delightful into explanation data from study programme that be conduct over the preceding ten years. The emphasis is on both internal school elements that affect the growth of thought and practice as well as external, broader contextual issues that may impede such changes. Many of the obstacles faced by learners are said to be caused by current paradigms of thought. (Ainscow, Mel, 2005)

Review of Literature

Despite official language that says both goals are complimentary, inclusion agenda. In order to ensure that all students succeed, the article emphasizes necessity to adopt a broader perspective of constitutes achievement. The paper draws on past works that have advanced the discussion in order to develop this assessment of current and existing inclusion programmes. The existing Code of Practice, according to this research, maintains a discrepancy model of the kid that is mainly conflict with addition ideals. (Glazzard, Jonathan.2013)

Inclusion has been difficult to define for academics working in the field of comprehensive education. It is frequently referred to process rather than a place or journey rather than an endpoint. Overcoming hurdles reference to the social representation of disability, which views disability as the end result of a person's interface with the social, political, and environmental barriers that avoid them access and participate in society. As long as latter can adapt to the consistent standard of such institutions, integration the procedure of including community with disabilities in already-existing conventional educational institution.(Graham, Linda J. 2020)Systemic change has not occurred, inclusive programmes can grow, albeit gradually. The article concludes by arguing that moral and ethical grounds require those working on inclusion to strive to include all children wherever it is necessary and that each person must first internalize the change within themselves. (Alur, Mithu,2001). Inclusive education in South Korea and its difficulties, prior to introducing pertinent policies for extraordinary and comprehensive education, the history of extraordinary education is first explained. The condition of inclusive education is then critically discussed based on the advantages and difficulties that teachers who are practicing inclusive education see. The conversation is expanded to cover more general topics and elements that have an impact on the implementation of inclusive education, such as teacher preparation programmes and the interactions between general and special educators. (Kim, Yong-Wook. 2014) promoting inclusive education In order to explore the effects of these reforms for various student groups, I study the policy changes in every country and analyze both aggregate and disaggregated assignment data in each setting. Results indicate that the various reform processes in each environment led to various student outcomes in every nation, with separation rising in Australia, falling in the USA. As students on the autism spectrum are further possible to incident educational separation or exclusion in both nations, data further show that the impact of these regulations have not be disseminated evenly across category. (De Bruin, Kate,2019) A shared growth process spread throughout the schools. It began with the disruption of established procedures and was supported by a variety of institutional and outside influences, including inclusion-related ideas. The "standards agenda" of the country had a significant impact on the paths that schools took. While it limited inclusive development, it also gave it a specific emphasis and encouraged schools to take into account challenges that may have otherwise been disregarded. (Ainscow, Mel, Tony Booth, and Alan Dyson 2006)

Conceptions of addition centre primarily on degree of engagement that kids with SEND and/or disabilities might attain, and how this might be impacted by the type of activity, the eminence of sustain, and the guidance opportunity that are available them. The article ends with a argument of the research's implication for teacher professional growth and school administration, with recommendations for particular implications for the practice of future PE instructors and teacher trainers. (Morley, David, et al.2005) In six schools across the United States, inclusive education held a series of focus group and interview with school administrator, universal and extraordinary educators, and associated service provider. Six themes emerge from the study, emphasize the value of defining comprehensive education as well as growing human capacity to know and apply the elements of comprehensive education system. These themes imply that effective leadership for inclusive education involves consideration of the systems and procedures in place to convey the idea that inclusive education serves as a foundational concept for all other practices. (Kozleski, Elizabeth B., et al,2015)The significance of inclusive education serves as the paper's theoretical foundation. In an effort to accomplish article discusses how Kenya, participant to international treaties education, have domestic numerous instrument into the Constitution as well as in other policy and legal frameworks. The article discusses the progress Kenya has achieved toward inclusive education, analyses difficulties Kenya is encountering throughout the implementation of inclusive education, and also offers solutions for bridging the gaps that have been found going forward. (Adoyo, Peter Oracha, and Michael Lumumba Odeny.2015)

The idea of comprehensive education and how viewed within confines of European countries' educational policies have misrepresented and are continually developing. A comprehensive approach to education for all students, regardless of age, is known as inclusive education. Its aim is to give all students admission to relevant, high-quality educational opportunity in their local community, beside their friends and peers. (Watkins, Amanda. 2017)

Inclusive and Strategic Leadership

The school's mission statement demonstrates its assurance to ideals of addition and diversity, which place a quality on equity and better learning outcome for all students. Every learner in the school should be able to access the mission statement in a variety of formats. The leadership team at the school promotes and exemplifies the ideals and reward of comprehensive education, with having high standards for every student. This is done in meeting, on school website, in school communications, during school meetings, and in regular face-to-face interactions. It is recommended to use the person's first language in all types of communication. The school leadership team collaborate initiatives for on the whole school improvement that are helpful to all students. This entails making short-, medium-, and long-term efforts to put the School expansion Plan's comprehensive educational methods into practice and to progress them. A secure physical environment and a favorable education environment are established by the school management team using a worldwide design approach to the school environment and prospectus.

Planning for Overall School Development

The school is dedicated to including all students. The mission statement, for example, reflects how inclusion ideals are defined made visible, and supporting all of the school's planning and practice activities. Through a targeted action plan, whole school development upholds best practice while growing inclusive opportunity for all the students. This is frequently evaluated and examined to make sure that inclusive practices are being followed. The School Management Team has to consistently assess how the action plans are being implemented throughout a system of current school self-evaluation. Parents obtain part in the development the overall growth of the school. Parents are given access to the full school growth plan and reports on its accomplishment and progress in a set-up they can understand.

Inclusive Environment Throughout the School

To offer a flexible and accessible learning environment for everyone, worldwide plan for education is to the school's environmental plan. The removal of physical obstacles to inclusion and the maintenance of best practices are addressed in an action plan. Additionally, staff training in the use of relevant techniques and tools must be part of this (such as evacuation chairs). Learning resources used in all subject areas, including handouts, books, charts, and other tools, reflect the diversity of the entire school community. In order to understand how the school community feels about wellbeing and inclusion on problems like harassment, curriculum, sexism, cultural sensitivity, etc., a periodic survey of the school environment is conducted.

Collaboration with Parents And Community Engagement

Parents are assisted by the school in finding community networks and options for help. As a result, local resources are recognized and used. In school, parents actively participate in advocacy, advising, and decision-making processes. Every donation is valued. During meetings, everyone's input is sincerely sought after, respected, and encouraged. At the school, areas are made where parents can gather. At the school, parents are seen participating in extracurricular activities and in the classroom. In order to better sustain their child's education at home and at the school, parents are given training chances to improve their parenting techniques.

Planning for Individual Education

High expectations for the student are a hallmark of individual educational planning, which also includes challenges that push learning while always assuring realistic goals. Identification, use, coordination, and management of the services and maintain resources accessible to students with Individual Educational requirements are all part of Individual Educational Planning. In order to assess learner requirements and create the Individual Educational Program, the school collaborates with families and other stakeholders as part of Individual Educational Planning. In the IEP process, the learner's input is solicited in various ways and to varying degrees. Although differentiated based on the needs of the learner, personality educational planning sets the teaching within an age-appropriate curricular structure. Individual educational planning, which incorporates visual, tactile, and kinesthetic resources as well as experiences, determines the customized teaching that educators deliver for a variety of learners' requirements.

Teaching and Learning

Through active, independent, and cooperative learning, education and learning activities are significant and properly demanding for various learners. They are connected to the goals, needs, and interests of the learner. All students have the chance to learn in a community of learners thanks to curriculum design. The flexibility of curriculum should utilize to allocate the instructor to plan a diversity of easily accessible and significant learning opportunity for all students. Collaboration between the teacher and LSE is used to create adaptations and differentiate instruction. Teachers give LSEs advance notice of work schedules and pertinent instructional materials so that they have enough time to make the necessary adjustments. Promoting, learner engagement, self-esteem, and a sense of competence, the development of strong relationships with students by class teams enables the communication of high expectations for each student. Together, educators and LSEs serve the interest students. Education is goal-oriented and prepares students to master successful cope mechanisms and deal with academic difficulties. Failures and errors are acknowledged, and growth from them is encouraged.

Learner and Staff Well Being

All students are encouraged to develop themselves holistically at the school, so their talents, knowledge, variety of ability, and various needs are recognized and met. Giving students the skills they need to overcome obstacles like poverty, mobility, unemployment, family stress, inequity, harassment, and aggression will help them become resilient, autonomous citizens. All students' voices are encouraged to be heard at school, and personal identities and experiences are encouraged to be expressed. With a strong pastoral care programme, the school promotes and protects the learners' wellbeing. The school welcomes diversity, and it is incorporated into all facets of the school community.

Continuous Professional Development

The involvement of school staff in professional and personal growth as well as training in all facets of comprehensive education is encouraged. opportunity are created for educator to collaborate, share resources, and experience education in order to discover novel approaches to addressing learner variety. There are options for professional development that can help teachers become more inclusive pedagogues (flexible teaching-learning approaches) and better serve the different needs of students. Since students who may have "invisible" disabilities run a higher risk of dropping out their circumstances go unreported in learning settings, educators receive training on how to recognize and assist these students. School administrators are aware of ingrained prejudices that might result in discriminatory behavior, and they help and support teachers as they identify and correct prejudice where it occurs. ICT can make it easier for learners of all backgrounds to participate in educational activities, fostering educational equity. All instructors should be encouraged to sign up for CPD courses with this focus.

Positive Behaviour Management

Following a consultation approach, a school-based behavior policy is created and accessible to all stakeholders (educators, students, and parents).School-based behavior policies are reflected in classroom and school rules, which are made apparent to all parties involved. Clear, concise regulations for the classroom and school should mirror the daily procedures of the institution. In order to enhance student behavior and school participation, schools implement school-wide positive behavior support techniques. At school, social and emotional literacy as well as positive behavior are encouraged. For students who are having trouble adhering to the school's behavior rules, reasonable modifications are made, and coping skills are encouraged.

Conclusion

The national inclusive education framework to schools on their journey towards inclusion how important it is for school administrators to foster a welcoming, inclusive environment that fosters learning for all students. Additionally, it motivates school administrators to address the various requirements of students and provide a productive learning environment. This theme is centered on the top priorities that educators within a learning environment determine throughout whole-school expansion plan. This structure promotes common involvement in the creation of priority target that incorporate addition of sustain for all learner as well as a common obligation to implement those priority targets. Throughout the application of worldwide plan for education, improved accessibility, and the elimination of curricular, social, and physical barriers to addition, this theme suggest creating an environment is conducive to inclusive learning. Additionally, it advises routine reviews of the academic programme, community, and physical environment. The responsibility of community members to actively participate in the school community, In order to support the students, the school works in conjunction with the parents to address parental engagement. The establishment, execution, and assessment of Individual Education Plans (IEPs) for all students who want support, It encourage the participation of all students who interact with the student in the planning, execution of the learning programme for them. It also implies the necessity of student contribution in the structure of education projects for network and assistance are also recommended.

References

- Ahsan, M. Tariq, and Jahirul Mullick. "The journey towards inclusive education in Bangladesh: Lessons learned." Prospects 43.2 (2013): 151-164.
- Azorín, Cecilia, and Mel Ainscow. "Guiding schools on their journey towards inclusion." International Journal of Inclusive Education 24.1 (2020): 58-76.
- Smyth, Fiona, et al. "Inclusive education in progress: policy evolution in four European countries." European Journal of Special Needs Education 29.4 (2014): 433-445.

- Kearney, Alison, and Ruth Kane. "Inclusive education policy in New Zealand: reality or ruse?." International Journal of Inclusive Education 10.02-03 (2006): 201-219.
- Lindsay, Geoff. "Inclusive education: a critical perspective." British journal of special education 30.1 (2003): 3-12.
- Polat, Filiz. "Inclusion in education: A step towards social justice." International Journal of Educational Development 31.1 (2011): 50-58.
- Ainscow, Mel. "Developing inclusive education systems: what are the levers for change?." Journal of educational change 6.2 (2005): 109-124.
- Glazzard, Jonathan. "A critical interrogation of the contemporary discourses associated with inclusive education in E ngland." Journal of Research in Special Educational Needs 13.3 (2013): 182-188.
- Graham, Linda J. "Inclusive education in the 21st century." Inclusive education for the 21st century. Routledge, 2020. 3-26.
- Alur, Mithu. "Some cultural and moral implications of inclusive education in India—A personal view." Journal of Moral Education 30.3 (2001): 287-292.
- Kim, Yong-Wook. "Inclusive education in South Korea." International journal of inclusive education 18.10 (2014): 979-990.
- De Bruin, Kate. "The impact of inclusive education reforms on students with disability: an international comparison." International journal of inclusive education 23.7-8 (2019): 811-826.
- Ainscow, Mel, Tony Booth, and Alan Dyson. "Inclusion and the standards agenda: negotiating policy pressures in England." International journal of inclusive education 10.4-5 (2006): 295-308.
- Morley, David, et al. "Inclusive physical education: Teachers' views of including pupils with special educational needs and/or disabilities in physical education." European Physical Education Review 11.1 (2005): 84-107.

- Kozleski, Elizabeth B., et al. "A never ending journey: Inclusive education is a principle of practice, not an end game." Research and Practice for Persons with Severe Disabilities 40.3 (2015): 211-226.
- Adoyo, Peter Oracha, and Michael Lumumba Odeny. "Emergent inclusive education practice in Kenya, challenges and suggestions." (2015).
- Watkins, Amanda. "Inclusive education and European educational policy." Oxford Research Encyclopedia of Education. 2017.

Dr. K. C. Lalithambika joined Jaya College of Arts and Science, Chennai which was the beginning of the journey and after a service, spanning 4 years, she moved to Thiruthangal Nadar College and she has been serving the Institution since 1999. She started as a Lecturer in English and headed the department from 2008 and was promoted as Vice -Principal in the year 2009 and is still working in the same capacity. Meanwhile she was blessed with an opportunity to work in the capacity of the Principal In-charge for a period of five and a half months which has given her a plethora of experiences. Her strong organizational skills and multi-tasking abilities as a team leader has helped a lot in the transition into administrative zone of work. The key role in the many facets of students' affairs and her overall supervision of the smooth functioning of the college which includes academic policy making, admission process and recruitment initiatives and so on has given her an edge as an able administrator.

• • •

CHAPTER VIII

Inclusive Curriculum Construction and Modern Pedagogies to Enhance the Fundamentals of English Language Skills for English as Second Language Learners

Dr. N. Ravikumar[1] and Dr. Masilamani C.[2]

[1]*Assistant Professor, Department of English, Kristu Jayanti College (Autonomous), K. Narayanapura, Kothanur, Bangalore, Karnataka-560077.*

[2]*Assistant Professor, Department of English, Kristu Jayanti College (Autonomous), K. Narayanapura, Kothanur, Bangalore, Karnataka-560077.*

Abstract

An inclusive educational system is the most effective method to ensure that all kids have an equal chance to learn and develop the fundamental skills they need to succeed in school. The term 'curriculum' is derived from the Latin word 'currere', which means 'a kind of itinerary to learning.' When using an inclusive curriculum, various needs, prior knowledge, interests, and learner characteristics are taken into consideration. It tries to accurately communicate that all students take part in cooperative and group learning exercises in the same classroom. All students have the same chance under this curriculum framework, regardless of their preferred methods of learning. It is crucial for the academic, physical, moral, and emotional development of the student. The comprehensive curriculum refers to all of the learning opportunities that students have in school, in the classroom, in the library, and elsewhere. The experiences that students have while taking part in different activities in the classroom, library, lab, workshop, and playground are all included in the inclusive curriculum. In the numerous unofficial interactions between teachers and pupils, this needs to be put into practice. This research paper discusses the key principles of inclusive curricular design as well as cutting-edge pedagogical techniques for fostering the development of the fundamental language abilities.

Keywords: Learning Experience, Classroom, Inclusive Learning, Pedagogical Methods and Language Skills.

Introduction

When creating educational systems and programmes for modern teaching and learning, it is important to consider the characteristics and basic needs of the learners. Learning about the factors that affect learning and the classroom setting is a necessary part of the inclusive teaching method. Various students interpret and comprehend knowledge presented to them in various ways. This frequently stems from their actual lived experiences, which are closely linked to their sense of social identity. Designing an inclusive curriculum involves both reacting to these factors and making a conscious effort to employ strategies that encourage enjoyable learning experiences among them.

Since the learners in the learning stream are a diverse group, they contribute experiences to the classroom that are indicative of their social standing and culture. Culture permeates learning, so taking into account issues relating to the social and cultural dimensions of task design, communication channels, and information structuring should be permitted when designing instructional environments if the needs of culturally diverse learners are to be met and the student is to be treated as a whole. This suggests that educational activities go beyond knowledge and skills to include other aspects of what it means to be a person in society and a method that recognises the complex biological, sociological, and psychological individuals who make up students.

The goal of inclusive education, according to inclusive design, should be to end social exclusion, which results from attitudes and behaviours towards diversity in race, socioeconomic class, ethnicity, religion, gender, and ability. In the same vein, Sturomski (1997) states that due to the information processing difficulties that students with learning disabilities often experience with learning, more than that their peers without learning disabilities are in need of effective learning strategies instruction. Further, he suggests:

Because of the nature of their learning difficulties, students with learning disabilities need to become strategic learners, not just haphazardly using whatever learning strategies or techniques they have developed on their own, but becoming consciously aware of what strategies might be useful in a given learning situation and capable of using those strategies effectively. (p. 4)

Language instruction should be focused on two-way process of transformation of knowledge and obtaining knowledge which balances both teaching and learning at the credit. In addition, Rubin (1996) believes that strategy instruction is a means of enhancing learners' procedural knowledge, which leads to more successful learning. She states, "Strategy instruction is one way to work towards enhancing your procedural knowledge. Since many adults are 'language phobic" or inexperienced with language learning, they need to gain more procedural knowledge to deflect negative affective influences and to begin to experience some success". (p. 151)

Curriculum Construction and Design

The obligation for curriculum design falls on educators in every area of learning. This fosters the success of all inclusive pupils. Based on students' educational, cultural, and social backgrounds, experiences, as well as physical or sensory impairment and mental health, an inclusive curriculum is constructed and designed. The different identities of the kids are recognised in inclusive curricula.

Their prior experiences mould it, and a variety of personal situations have an impact on how people learn. It is promoted as a way to eliminate obstacles, enhance results, and end discrimination.

The choice of course materials is crucial when creating a course. The manners of students are expected to demonstrate their learning components as well as the instructors' instructional strategies. Some students may benefit from the course while others may suffer. Hence, we must make sure kids can interact successfully with technologies, peer groups, educators, and supporting learning resources in order to promote inclusive learning. This means that identifying any obstacles to learning that the learning encounters may present is crucial to ensuring inclusive learning. The guidelines that follow must be all-inclusive.

Principles of Inclusive Curriculum Construction

Principles of Child Centeredness: It is mainly meant for the inclusive children only. So, while constructing the curriculum the child's age, interest, capability, capacity, aspiration, needs, physiology and psychology of the learner should be considered.

Principle of Community-Centeredness: It is to develop the society. So, social needs and regional needs of the learners should be counted.

Principle of Balance: It should produce the children who are not biased and having any inhibition. It should make the children to lead a balanced social life.

Principle of Need: Learner is left to face many challenges to face in the life. He has to be intellectually strong. He needs to get a good joy. He needs to perform all the duties that he is entrusted with both in family life and social life.

Principle of Utility: It should provide the child to lead a happy life. Hence, it should give the child rich experiences, both academic and social life.

Principle of Creativity: In today's competitive world one has to be creative for a sustained meaningful life. So, curriculum should help in developing creativity in the children.

Principle of Variety: Students are with different caliber in knowledge, traditions, intelligence, ability, aptitude and attitude.

Principle of Flexibility: Curriculum should not be rigid. It should be flexible according to the need of the learners.

Principle of Contemporary Knowledge: It should give enough knowledge about the contemporary life.

The curriculum planners make an effort to provide a thorough and application-focused curriculum for all learners. There are undoubtedly a few challenges that make it difficult to achieve the curriculum's goals. As we attempt to address all social issues and needs, external influences are inescapable. People frequently, even teachers, criticise the school and its curriculum. When someone says the curriculum is irrelevant, they indicate that the learners won't gain too lot from learning it.

Based on the requirements of the inclusive learner, the instructional strategies are planned. This should be examined in terms of the curriculum and the pupils' knowledge levels. It is the responsibility of the teachers to advance the students to a desired level, and this is only feasible with an effective curriculum. It should adhere to specific goals, accepted textbooks, and a good evaluation mechanism. For everyone's future success, inclusive curricula should be adaptable and take into account each learner's interest, level of comprehension, and performance.

Pedagogical Methods for Inclusive Learning

The objectives for which it is taught dictate the instructional strategies. When choosing a method to teach a foreign language like English, more consideration must be used. Indian educators firmly believe that the purpose of English instruction in India is to equip pupils to master the language practically. In order to accomplish this goal, we must use a variety of techniques and strategies. We emphasised the significance of the relationship between the objectives of teaching and the teaching strategies by stating that 'the question,' 'what should be taught,' and 'how should be taught,' are closely related because, when the best strategies for teaching are developed, more can be learned from them. The following strategies, tactics, and approaches were widely used in inclusive classroom.

Grammar Translation Method

The oldest method is called 'grammar translation,' in which teachers translate every word, phrase, and sentence from English into the pupils' native tongues. It was simple for both teachers and students since the kids were able to assimilate English phraseology through the medium of their mother tongue thanks to the teacher's translation of every word, phrase, and sentence from English into their mother tongue. It places a strong emphasis on learning grammar, which is done through presenting and studying grammatical rules, or deductively. The mother tongue's grammatical structures are contrasted with those of the foreign language. This approach allows for the elegant acquisition of grammar skills by all learners.

Advantages of GTM in Inclusive Classroom

- Child proceeds from known to unknown in Grammar Translation method.
- Vocabulary and the language using ability in mother tongue help the learners to learn English easily. It helps in building vocabulary.
- Translation from English into the mother tongue enables the learners to develop their vocabulary very rapidly.
- This method avoids difficult definitions or lengthy explanations, the learners are able to grasp the exact meaning of words.
- The teachers don't need to labor hard either in the preparation lesson plan or in the process of implementing the teaching items in the class. He doesn't need to think of the ways and means to explain new words even without using audio-visual aids.
- Comprehension is easily tested.
- Testing the students' comprehending ability in English is easy as they are permitted to tell the answer in their mother tongue.
- Proper grammar is taught easily. English grammar is taught very easily by comparing it with the grammar of the mother tongue.

(*MMIT* 129)

Direct Method

The direct method of instruction emphasizes the direct correlation between lived experience and verbal, aural, and contextual expression. The options for learning the fundamentals of language are also numerous. The primary goal of the Direct Method is to teach any foreign language through dialogue, reading, and writing in the target language while connecting the experience to the language and avoiding the use of the students' L1. With the aid of their peers and instruction from the class teacher, students using this method can express their opinions on the subject matter in a second language.

Advantages of DM in Inclusive Classroom

- Natural way of leaning any language is in the order of Listening, Speaking, Reading and Writing.
- Fluency of speech is guaranteed and students are involved in conversation in English, their oral fluency in improved.
- The students are making to listen to their teachers and then to speak, they have a good model to pronounce English words. This practice helps them developing a better English pronunciation.
- Fluency in speech helps in written work. Only thing that the students have to concentrate is to mind on their spelling.
- Promotes the study of literature. The students are able to further proceed to enjoy literature with the knowledge their gained in oral and written aspects of the target language. (*MMIT* 136)

Dr. West's New Method

Dacca University professor Dr. Michael West He is the creator of this innovative approach of teaching English. He developed his own approach to teaching English after becoming unhappy with the other methods already in use. This approach took into account the pupils' anxieties about studying and trying to acquire English. Dr. West has given reading a lot of weight in his new approach.

He was adamant that Indian pupils should focus on reading aloud in addition to practicing silent reading. The articulatory system of the students will work quickly when practicing reading. By using this strategy, students can improve their reading comprehension, pronunciation, stress and intonation, and highly key linguistic vocabularies.

Advantages of Dr. West New Method in Inclusive Classroom

- The teaching of English should develop the feeling of internationalism and help in establishing relationship with the other countries and broaden their outlook.
- English is a rich language and a good number of literatures in science and technology shall help Indian students.
- Children up to the age 12 should be kept busy in reading only. Acquiring reading efficiency at the small age is easy. This character of the children needs to be capitalized in the study of a foreign language.
- He didn't propose the art of speaking in his new method. Dr. West's New Method of Teaching is based on the psychological principle that the child tries to hear and understand before speaking. (*MIMT* 153)

Multidimensional Teaching Approach

Adult foreign language instruction necessitates careful consideration of psychological techniques due to the possibility that learning may have negative effects on adults' confidence and self-esteem. Nonetheless, there should be some controlled techniques to merge the usage of verbal and mechanical methodologies. As was mentioned in the preview section, pupils' cognitive and mental abilities were not met by behavioral techniques to teaching languages. The theoretical foundation weakened when new techniques like the communicative approach, lexical approach, and inductive procedures were introduced. This approach's two general human origins physical and mental are taken into consideration. The researcher uses the term 'physical' to refer to all physical elements of learning and teaching, including linguistically oriented approaches, teaching tools, and educational setting-related tactics. The researcher uses the term 'mental aspect' to refer to all activities associated with the human mind and how it functions. Every feature necessitates control over a particular mental activity.

Suggested Approaches for Inclusive Learning

A wide phrase, 'approach,' refers to a particular model based on study or theory. It is a perspective on education and learning. Any approach to teaching a language is based on a theoretical understanding of what language is and how it can be learned. This theoretical understanding then inspires teaching strategies, or the ways in which a subject is taught, that make use of classroom activities or techniques to aid all students in learning language skills. The inclusive classroom system can adapt the following strategies.

Structural Approach

The Structural Approach makes advantage of circumstances where meaning expresses itself in its final form. It is considered a structural method because the primary focus is on understanding sentence and phrase structures and patterns, as well as unique linguistic characteristics that facilitate sentence building, like word order and structural terms. At the first stages of this method, mother tongue is permitted primarily for explaining a circumstance when a certain sentence pattern needs to be practiced. Because the same theme is presented in various ways across languages, it is not possible to translate the structure that is intended to be used. The structures are practiced with the students until they are accustomed to them. The primary goal of this method is to provide the students with LSRW abilities so they can improve the foundation of their English through drills, achieve mastery of a crucial vocabulary, grammar, and writing, and place an emphasis on the aural-oral method.

Advantages of Structural Approach

- This approach, promotes speech habits of students with repeated oral drills for various structural patterns.
- Oral practice ensures that the students acquire proper pronunciation.
- If the teacher is innovative and create a better classroom situation, structural approach can motivate the students to the maximum.
- Through habit formation structures are permanently grasped.
- It is best suited approach for objective based teaching of a foreign language.
- Proper selection and gradation of the learning material is possible through this approach.
- The class is always active as it encourages participation of all students.
- The free situation available in the classroom facilitates the functional aspects of the language.
- The popularity of the structural syllabus all over the country is the testimony of its effectiveness.
- Instant correction of students' mistakes is possible as its main emphasis is on oral practice of the language structures. (*MMIT* 169)

Communicative Approach

The Communicative approach to education emphasises the necessity of genuine dialogue for learning to occur. The four principles of linguistic competency, various linguistic forms, language use techniques, and social context can be the basis of an inclusive classroom system. These ideas can help people improve their speaking abilities.

Linguistic Competence: The learner who has the linguistic competence alone will be able to utilize the language to use as and when he requires.

Different Forms of Linguistics: The learner has to be acquainted with all the forms of linguistics. Only when he is familiar with different forms of linguistics, he will be able to choose the specific form to be used in a specific situation.

Strategies of Using the Language: The learner should possess all the skills that facilitate the learning of language. To be an effective use of language, he/she should be trained in different strategies which could be applied for using the language in different situations.

Social Background: English is taught as an L2, which implies that students must use it in social settings. The proverbial man is well-known for his company. In this method, a person will only exhibit interest in learning the target and applying it to the society when the atmosphere is appropriate. The student should be able to put his new knowledge into practise in society. The speaker should talk in a language that meets the audience's needs. Only then is he considered to have correctly used the language.

Advantages of Communicative Approach

- It provides for the teaching of everyday, real-world language used in variety of socio-cultural situations in which features of pronunciation, vocabulary, grammar and culture are selected and graded according to their priority in actual communication.
- It recognizes that the students must have a real purpose for using language.
- The language user feels satisfied with owns performance and that acts as a motivating factor.
- He is recognized the society where he uses the language successfully.
- It aims at giving practical aspect of using the language.
- It is situational, meaningful, motivating others and self-rewarding. (*MMIT* 181)

Communicative Language Teaching (CLT)

Learning a language is mostly done so that we can communicate with others and ourselves. Whichever language we learn should concentrate on the best practices for using it for communication. One needs to be fluent in all facets of the language, with linguistics being the most crucial. Only when both the speaker and listener are physically present and are aware of the situation can verbal communication take place. Words and structural elements are both necessary for effective communication. The internalization of strategies for developing proper behavior is a component of this strategy that focuses on the cognitive side. These programmes primarily draw on the inclusive learning approach when it comes to language use. Grammar rules, methods for choosing vocabulary, and social customs governing speech are all included. The behavioral component entails automating these strategies in order to translate them into fluid performance in real time. This mostly happens through repetition in transforming plans into performance.

Eclectic Approach or Integrated Approach

Eclectic refers to a free choice and acceptance of elements from diverse sources. No way is better than another and no method is worse. Every technique has advantages and disadvantages. No approach is flawless and entirely acceptable. This is our understanding based on the research and evaluation we have done thus far of various English teaching strategies. Depending on the dynamics of the class, the instructor is most qualified to choose the approach. He can use a variety of the techniques that have been presented so far as a compromise. Even in some instances, some teachers might employ techniques that haven't been widely publicized. The teacher's approach should only be used to improve the four language skills for the students. The focus should be on language abilities in the LSRW system's natural order. Various exercises are recommended in the recommended curriculum to practice speaking skill development. It is possible to use the question answer method. When necessary, a teacher may only explain some abstract terms, phrases, or circumstances in their mother tongue.

To teach grammar, the teacher might employ both inductive and deductive methods. He must watch out that the grammar lessons don't turn them against the English language. This is primarily due to the disdain that the majority of us feel for the English language, which we tried to learn after learning the grammar rules. There, creating a significant barrier to our language development. The learner like the play-way approach greatly, therefore the teacher can apply it. Whenever possible, appropriate audiovisual aids should be employed for learning. To achieve his goals of teaching English, the instructor must adapt his methods to the requirements and abilities of his students, as well as the time, resources, and tools at his disposal. We can call this as eclectic approach or complete approach or an integrated approach.

Total Physical Response

Based on these experiences, James Asher created Total Physical Reaction (TPR). The foundation of this approach is the integration of words and motion. The teacher issues commands and the students follow them. Within an hour of instruction, the students acquire 12 to 36 new words. Instructors are counseled to handle students' errors sympathetically, much like a parent. Lessons on Whole Physical Reaction employ a variety of posters, realizes, etc. Lessons can be taught without the use of teaching and learning materials at first. A teacher may use materials found in the classroom as students advance in their competency. According to Aggarwal's observations, "learning a language should be stress-free; learning a language activates the right hemisphere of the brain; and, in general, language is learned through listening." (78) We can set up an inclusive classroom system based on the aforementioned, and the students enthusiastically engaged in the activities. Once students began to enjoy learning, they naturally improved their linguistic abilities. Those who are just starting out and younger students favor this method.

Advantages of Total Physical Response

- TPR is criticized for being suitable only for beginner level learners.
- The teacher need not prepare too much to teach the lesson.

- Mixed ability class benefits more.
- It uses the participatory approach.
- It is useful for teaching learners with dyslexia. (*MMIT* 176)

Multilingual Pedagogical Approach

Depending on the students, the curriculum, and the teaching environment, it is a collection of concepts that are used to varying degrees in different approaches or ways. First, professors assist students in using their existing knowledge in this method. Second, when learning a new language, students draw on their prior knowledge. Lastly, students assess and, to the extent possible, transfer previously used learning strategies to a new language learning situation. It alludes to one's native tongue. Language learners must initially study in their native tongue before learning additional languages while in school. The students are able to switch between their L1 and L2 or other languages. Their sociocultural as well as inclusive cultural experiences are brought into the classroom and linked to the study of a second foreign language. The critical pedagogy of Freire, the scaffolding of Lev Vygotsky, the theory of cognition of Piaget, and the Gramscian philosophy of education serve as the cornerstones of multilingual education. In order to develop their curriculum and limit theoretical hegemony, MLE consults the community.

Constructive Approach

This strategy signifies the transition from behaviorism-based education to cognitive theory-based education. Active learning is made possible by constructivism, where students create their own meaning and build their own understanding of an idea throughout a class. Learning how to take initiative for their own learning experiences is one of the key goals of constructivist teaching. It encourages individualization of learning and autonomy and is learner-centered. Collaboration, creation, projects, and self-teaching are all encouraged in action-oriented constructivist language learning. It fosters understanding of learning, linguistics, and cross-cultural issues. It is comprehensive with a focus on content and a challenging learning environment.

Thematic Learning Approach

TLA places focus on a particular theme for a notion or concepts. Information is integrated into this and used to illustrate the subject. With the use of this technique, students can identify how vocabulary, tenses, structures, and other aspects of language are used throughout a range of subject matter. Thematic learning enables students to learn contextually and comprehensively, and they can relate their classroom assignments to real-world circumstances. It is experiential education. Thematic education takes into account the aptitude and interests of the students. It encourages cooperation among the diverse group.

Flipped Classroom Technique

Fundamentally, the flipped classroom model entails encouraging students to study for the subject in advance of class. As a result, the classroom is transformed into a lively setting where students expound on what they have already learned. Students research a subject at home so that any questions they may have can be addressed in class the following day. This enables pupils to venture outside of their comfort zones and pursue their inherent curiosities.

Design Thinking Technique

The foundation of this approach is the use of group analysis, brainstorming, creativity, and new ideas to solve real-world problems. Although the "design thinking technique" is a systematic pedagogy, it can be extremely messy in practice because certain problems may not have a solution. Yet, the Case Method fosters students' curiosity, critical thinking abilities, and creativity while preparing them for life in the real world. This method is frequently employed in well-known MBA or masters courses to study actual problems that firms have faced in the past. The Design Thinking School was established by Design Thinking proponent Ewan McIntosh as a part of his 'No Tosh' consulting team. The 'No Tosh' uses some of the top media and technology organizations in the world to coach instructional strategies for the notion. Design Thinking for Educators also offers teachers with an online toolkit with directions to reconnoiter design thinking in any classroom system.

Gamification Techniques

One of the teaching methods that have been investigated, particularly in elementary and preschool education, is learning through the use of games. Students learn through games without even recognising it. As a result, 'Gamification' or learning via play is a teaching method that can be very effective at any age. Also, it's a great way to keep pupils engaged. In order to motivate children further, teachers should create projects that are age- and knowledge-appropriate for their pupils while also being visually appealing. One possibility is to encourage students to design online tests on a particular subject. Students might compete against one another to see who performs better on a test. In this way, students can enjoy the competition with peers while also having fun and learning.

Communicative Language Teaching (CLT)

The evolution of the British language teaching tradition starting in the late 1960s is where Communicative Language Teaching (CLT) got its start. It is the outcome of the American rejection of audio-lingualism. Numerous strategies and methods for teaching English help students pick up some of the language. Our students, however, exhibit considerable reluctance when speaking in English. The English language learners' ability to communicate in English is taken care of via communicative language teaching.

Instead of the teacher's monologue, conversation in English classes should be encouraged. The majority of the exercises involve group or pair work. The methods used to perform the lessons include role playing, language games, grammar games, interactive sessions, interviews, debates, and other pertinent exercises. Textbooks are not the only source of educational material. For designing, activities, and problem-solving, any materials are used, even unusual ones. Some educators choose any news item from the Hindu, prepare a few questions, read the questions aloud to the class, or write the questions on the board. They then have a brief pre-reading session with the class before reading the news item to the class so that the students can respond to the questions. Due to the fact that the students listen in order to understand the news item, this has evolved into a very effective activity for improving both reading and listening skills. Some professors take advantage of their pupils' enthusiasm for cricket by letting them watch games, assigning them to read about the sport the next day in the Hindu, and facilitating brief discussions. By using this strategy, you can learn a lot of vocabulary.

Cooperative Language Learning (CLL)

A more comprehensive teaching strategy known as Collaborative Learning includes cooperative language learning. With exercises requiring pair and group work, cooperative learning provides the most learning. "Cooperative learning is group; learning activity organized so that learning is dependent on the socially structured exchange of information between learners in groups and in which each learner is held accountable for his or her own learning and is motivated to increase the learning of others", (117) defined Christopher in his definition of the term. Group activities are a key component of cooperative learning and are included in a thorough theory and framework for the use of group work in instruction. Group activities are judiciously planned that can ensure supreme participation of the students to each other's learning.

Task-Based Language Teaching (TBLT)

Learning a language is different from really picking up the language. The process of picking up a language is largely automatic, whereas language learning is largely deliberate. Other targeted languages are taught as the mother tongue is acquired. Learning a language is preferable to acquisition. In this approach, students in English classes should have the chance to learn the language. It ought to provide a setting that is conducive to English language learning. The activities in the English classroom must be engaging in addition to providing a conducive environment for learning English. The English teacher's sole choice to meet this requirement right now is to use a task-based language teaching approach. Willis say that: the educational framework known as "Task-Based Language Teaching (TBLT) is for the theory and practise of teaching second or foreign languages. It is based on a confluence of concepts drawn from educational philosophy, theories of second language acquisition, actual research on successful teaching methods, and the demands of language learning in modern culture" (45).

Advantages of Task-Based Language Teaching

- There are many advantages of Task-Based Language Teaching (TBLT) for the learners of English as a second language.
- The most important benefit of TBLT is that it removes the passivity in the minds of the learners and act as a motivational for learning more.
- The learners stand to bring their experience for completing the tasks which ensures that the learners are able to execute their knowledge in using situation. And, of course, teachers are there to help them in this regard.
- Task-Based learning is advantageous to the student because it is more student-centred, allows for more meaningful communication, and often provides for practical extra-linguistic skill building.
- Teacher may present language in the pre-task, the students are ultimately free to use what grammar constructs and vocabulary they want. (*MMIT* 144)

As meaning is given top priority, kids will become interested and voluntarily participate in more activities that promote language acquisition. Language forms can be used whichever learners like. So, the students are not subjected to the strict stigma that permeates an English class. The learners are not completing tasks in any staged or manufactured scenario because tasks relate to real-world activity. The type of task to which learners can give their complete attention while adding language aspect to the sense they have in their head and heart is a real-life scenario. In this approach,

TBLT exercises will work as a catalyst for enthusiastically acquiring the target language.

In a task-based language teaching class, completing the task's objective takes precedence. The results of tasks are used to evaluate them. TBLT offers a well-organized framework for both training and evaluation. Tasks serve as the fundamental building blocks of syllabus design, enabling instructors to plan lectures, evaluate their effectiveness, and set up a framework that feels reasonably authentic for students to interact with one another. The ability to concentrate on what they are saying to each other rather than how they are saying it is most crucial.

The potential for 'natural' learning inside the classroom is provided through task-based education. Although it may accommodate language form, it prioritizes meaning above form. It has internal motivation. Although it supports a learner-centered educational philosophy, it also permits instructor input and guidance. It supports the growth of communicative fluency without sacrificing accuracy. It can be used in conjunction with a more conventional strategy.

Activity Based Learning (ABL)

In Activity-based learning (ABL) teaching method, in the words of Dhand "students actively participate in the learning experience rather than sit as passive listeners" (114). Learning activities if based on real life experience help learners to transform knowledge or information into their personal knowledge which they can apply in different situations. Activity based learning as the learning process in which "student is actively involved in doing or in seeing something done." (123) Activity Based Teaching (ABT) method "frequently involves the use of manipulative materials" (124). According to Sharma, "ABL helps learners to construct mental models that allow for 'higher-order' performance such as applied problem solving and transfer of information and skills" (179). In ABL, the learner considers the learning objectives and considers how to approach an issue that is presented to him. Instead than learning about the material, the students learn how to approach an issue. They gain knowledge about the subject matter as they work to solve the issue. Without students' motivation, teaching and learning cannot be done effectively. Hake contends that motivating pupils through interactive activities is an efficient and practical way to teach difficult ideas. He emphasizes the significance of many pursuits associated with the ideas being put out.

Conclusion

Beckman (2002) points out that when students with learning disabilities become strategic learners, they become productive lifelong learners, and as a result of strategy use, they

trust their own minds, know that there's more than one right way to do things, acknowledge their mistakes, evaluate their products and behaviour, feel a sense of power, and know how to try.

(p. 17) Focusing on learner groups who may be at risk of marginalization, exclusion, or underachievement is a key component of inclusion. This suggests that there is a moral obligation to support those groups that are statistically the most vulnerable and, where required, to take action to secure their presence, participation, and success in the educational system. The Floe project is directed by the Inclusive Design Research Centre, which also offers tools, advice, and guidelines for generating learning resources with inclusive designs, such as inclusive web games and simulations. In order to help educators learn about and incorporate Inclusive Design ideas, processes, and tools into the design process, Floe has produced an inclusive design handbook. The development of such tools might improve inclusive design methods. Numerous academics also advised instructional designers to start the process of developing culturally inclusive designs by implementing the social constructivist learning methodology. Recognizing how learning is influenced by culture and society grounds the design process in the communities and people for whom the learning products are designed. The need to concentrate explicitly on how educational policy and practise can improve both the acknowledgment given to historically marginalized groups and at the same time provide representation and participatory access is suggested by equity issues about social inclusion with reference to education.

References

* Aggarwal. J. C. *Principles, Methods & Techniques of Teaching.* Vikas Publishing House Pvt Ltd. 2008.
* Beckman, P. (2002). *Strategy instruction.* Arlington, VA: ERIC Clearinghouse on Disabilities and Gifted Education, Council for Exceptional Children. [ERIC Document Number: ED474302]. Available at: http://www.eric.ed.gov/
* Bennett, W. A. *Aspects of Language and Language Teaching.* Cambridge University Press.1969
* Candlin C.N. Syllabus design as a critical process. In Brumfit C.J. (ed.) *General English Syllabus Design: Curriculum and Syllabus Design for The General English Classroom. ELT Documents 118.* Pergamon Press.1984.
* Chauhan, S. S. *Innovations in Teaching Learning Process.* Vikas Publishing House Pvt. Ltd. 2008.
* Christopher, S. W.*Computer and Language Learning.* SEAMEO – Regional Language Centre.1998
* Dhand, H. *Techniques of Teaching.* APH Publishing Corporation. 2009.
* Lee, W. R. *Language teaching games and contexts.* Oxford University Press.1976
* Krishnaswamy and Lalitha Krishnaswamy. *Teaching English–Approaches, Methods and Techniques.* Macmillan India Ltd.2003.
* Nunan D. *Developing Tasks for the Communicative Classroom.* Cambridge University Press. 1989.
* Prabhu N.S. *Second Language Pedagogy: A Perspective.* Oxford University Press. 1987.
* Rubin, J. Study of cognitive processes in second language learning. *Applied Linguistics,* 11,
* 117-131. 1981

- Ravikumar, N. *Modern Methods and Innovative Techniques in English Language Teaching for Indian Students,* Non-Olympic Times Publication House, 2019.
- Siddiqui, M.H. *Techniques of Classroom Teaching.* APH Publishing Corporation.2009.
- Sharma, R. N. *Principles and Techniques of Education.* Surjeet Publications.2008.
- ---,*Contemporary Teaching of English.* Surjeet Publications.2008.
- Sturomski, Neil. *Interventions for students with learning disabilities.* National Information Center for Children and Youth with Disabilities, Washington. 1997 [ED 415 607]
- Willis J. *A Framework for Task-Based Learning.* Longman.1996.
- Wright, A. *Visual Material for the Language Teacher.* Longman. 1977.

---

[1]**Dr. N. Ravikumar**, Assistant Professor, Department of English, Kristu Jayanti College (Autonomous) K. Narayanapura, Kothanur, Bangalore, Karnataka-560077. He has 7 years of teaching experience. His areas of specializations are Children and Myth Literature, Indian Writing in English, Literary Criticism and Theory, and English Language Teaching.

[2]**Dr. Masilamani C**, Assistant Professor, Department of English, Kristu Jayanti College (Autonomous) K. Narayanapura, Kothanur, Bangalore, Karnataka-560077. He has more 10 years of teaching experience. His areas of specializations are Indian Writing in English, Literary Criticism and Theory, and English Language Teaching.

• • •

CHAPTER IX

The Regressive Effects of Child Abuse and its Constructive Solution through Torey Hayden's One Child

Dr. Pauline V. N.[1] and Ms. Daffline Gladson[2]

[1]Assistant Professor, Department of English, Kristu Jayanti College (Autonomous), Bengaluru

[2]MSc Clinical Psychology (IYear) in Kristu Jayanti College (Autonomous), Bengaluru

---

Abstract

Malevolence and abuse against little children have been prevalent in the world for ages. But child abuse as a social problem has gained attention and was documented only from the late 60s of this century. Scientists and psychologists have done varied studies in this field and have given enough evidence on the widespread occurrence of child abuse in different forms all over the world. This paper focuses on the book *One Child* by Torey Hayden, which talks about child abuse undergone by a little girl called Sheila which made her violent, and uncooperative eventually leading to maladaptive conduct and mannerisms, also how the affection and attention of a loving teacher changed her life from the bad situation she had been in, to a better one. It also transforms her character and makes her sociable and ends with a positive note.

Key words: abuse, violence, maladaptive conduct

Introduction

Abusing a child physically and sexually is like murdering the innocence of a child at a very tender age. Maltreatment of little children is one of the most prevalent forms of child abuse in society worldwide. Neglect and child abuse can lead to major health issues and negative childhood experiences. Long-term damaging effects on a child's welfare, prospects, and health are possible. This issue includes any instances of abuse or neglect of a child under the age of eighteen by a parent, guardian, or other person with custody that causes harm or raises the risk of damage. Physical abuse is the willful application of force that may cause bodily harm. Examples include using force against a kid by beating, kicking, shaking, burning, or in other ways. Female children who experience sexual abuse and atrocities are never likely to have a normal, happy, or healthy life since, in the majority of the situations, the male family members who were meant to be guarding them betray their trust and sense of security. Not only do they lose their innocence but also the trust factor which leads them into facing a lot of short and long-term consequences. When we look at the short-term outcomes the sufferer normally goes through bouts of tantrums like fiery rage, malevolence, animosity, inferiority complex, bitterness ,inappropriate sexual behavior, hurting others, low academic performance, substance abuse, etc. Long-term effects may lead to stress, depression, sexual abuse of others who are vulnerable, suicidal tendencies, dysfunctional parenthood, drug abuse, alcoholism, unemployment, etc. These characteristic traits exemplify how a sexually abused child can perpetuate these bad qualities into her life and continue this dangerous cycle.

The author of the book *One Child*, Torey L. Hayden was born on May 21, 1951, in Livingston, Montana, in the United States. She is a special education teacher, a university lecturer, and a writer of non-fiction books based on her real-life experiences with teaching and counselling children with disabilities and children who exhibit mannerism and behavioral challenges. She has also written few fiction books. Her works mostly tackle issues in the field of her expertise, such as selective mutism, fetal alcohol syndrome, sexual abuse, autism, and Tourette syndrome.

In *One Child*, Torey Hayden projects herself not just as a teacher but also as a compassionate individual who caters to the emotional needs of a problematic student. This book gives comfort, hope, and motivation to the reader and also to people who have lost hope in life due to abuse. It proves that patience and loving interactions with challenging kids will improve their confidence and make them better children. Reading about the successful results in Hayden's class offers a cause for optimism for children who are deprived of love and hail from troubled family backgrounds and provides them the will to act to change them.

Hayden stands out for her compassionate treatment of young children who have had horrific events in their lives. She believes in strong emotional ties and human interactions which could transform a troubled individual into a better human being. Her life narratives specifically highlight the strength of emphasizing the interconnectedness and psychological impact on an abused child.

Torey Hayden's non-fiction narratives detail her experience as a child psychologist and as a teacher who serves the needs of children who come from difficult homes. Her books are first-person narratives of her experiences working with and instructing kids that exhibit emotional and dysfunctional behaviours. Her experiences provide readers a perspective of what life is really like and enables one to consider the benefits, challenges, and hurdles of teaching children who are in crisis. Her writings show how difficult these circumstances may be and how limited and frustrating the achievements and the level of success can be. Nevertheless, she also offers hard-won joy and optimism in little or huge doses.

The narratives of Hayden stress on the interpersonal interactions and emotional ties that come along while working with problematic kids. Her life narratives emphasize the positive connections between a teacher and her emotionally disturbed students and provide a special voice to the feminine side of the human experience as well as the importance of relationships, emotion, and intuition in everyday life.

The first chapter of *One Child* introduces us to Hayden, a special education teacher. She reads a newspaper article about a six-year-old girl who had burned and abused a three-year-old child a few days prior. It happens so, that the girl did not have a suitable room in the hospital and was put in Hayden's class for the time being. In the beginning Sheila hardly ever talked since her parents had mistreated and abandoned her, but eventually participated in more of Hayden's class activities throughout the course of the following five months. Hayden was gradually able to uncover more information about Sheila's past, which included horrifying sexual abuse at the hands of an uncle.

Hayden helped Sheila in *One Child*, to get over her mother's abandonment which resulted in the child's feelings of worthlessness, shame, humiliation, neglect and hatred.

'My mama take me out on the road and leave me there. She push me out of the car and I fall down so's a rock cutted up my leg right here. See."

"My mama don't love me so good"

"My mama take Jimmie and go to California. That be where they live now. Jimmie he be my brother and he be four years old, 'cept that he only be two when my Mama she leave. I aint't seen Jimmie in two whole years" (*One Child*, p-94)

Maladaptive Mannerism

Maladaptive mannerism refers to any actions that prevent a person from participating in or adjusting to new living circumstances. Though intended to lessen or prevent stress, these practises are typically upsetting and might eventually result in increased difficulty, discomfort, and concern.

Many individuals unknowingly develop unhealthy coping strategies to handle worry, stress, or panic attacks. These methods are employed because they momentarily alleviate discomfort, yet they are disruptive by nature.

However, taking unhelpful measures won't help one deal with the root cause of their worry. The momentary relief that these acts provide typically just serves as a stepping stone to new issues or an exacerbation of existing ones.

Reasons for Maladaptive Mannerism:

Maladaptive mannerism is a conduct that hinders a person's capacity to operate in daily life or cope with challenging circumstances due to the problems like sexual or physical abuse that he or she has undergone or going through and also acts as a let out for their suppressed emotions. It deviates considerably from what would be predicted as the developmental stage of the person. These actions are frequently risky and disruptive. They are typically viewed as disobedience or poor kid conduct. In order to improve their actions, youngsters are frequently chastised rather than supported.

The majority of maladaptive actions are coping strategies meant to lessen uncomfortable feelings and heighten pleasant ones, but in practice, they frequently fail. A youngster selects a tactic from the available options and learns by experiencing the results. They are encouraged to use a tactic that enables them to achieve their objective of lessening uncomfortable sensations or boosting good emotions. A strategy's likelihood of being used again will decrease if it fails to meet this objective. This kind of emotionally-driven reinforcement learning process typically has additional detrimental effects.

Maladaptive Psychology in *One Child*

Maladaptive mannerism prevent one from adjusting to unfamiliar or challenging situations. They may begin following a significant life change, sickness, or traumatic experience. It can also be a mannerism pattern that you developed at a tender age.

Maladaptive habits can be recognised, and they can be changed for more beneficial ones. If not, they may result in emotional breakdown, social, and health issues. There are remedies if things are getting out of hand. A trained therapist will be able to handle one going through these issues related to mannerism and make their life better by helping them face the obstacles in life with necessary guidance and support. It affects people of all age groups and socioeconomic backgrounds recognizing it and working to alter it are the keys to transformation.

There is huge difference between adaptive and maladaptive mannerism. Mostly life does not unfold as planned. One can choose to adapt to a challenging situation or might give in to the enormity of trouble. It may not be a deliberate decision at the time. It can only be a momentary reaction while we give it some thought. Making a decision to fix a problem or lessen an undesirable effect is adaptive mannerism. In order to adjust to the circumstance, a person might find a way to escape it or do something that he specifically did not want to do. An avid dancer who loses a leg in an accident can, for example, decide to keep dancing while attempting to adapt by using an artificial limb; this is known as adaptive mannerism. Maladaptive conduct is the act of ignoring a loss or the necessity for adjustment. It appears terrible and out of control when one considers it.

Maladaptive mannerism can lead to substantial and enduring effects in addition to getting criticism from family, school, and employment. Alienation is one of the foremost effects of maladaptive mannerism. Children who exhibit maladaptive mannerisms throughout their formative years will not build strong connections and may find it difficult to earn the respect or regard of their elders. The typical tendency of children with this disorder is that; they show signs of laziness, unruliness, contempt, lack of attention etc. while, in reality, most of these are almost never the case. Instead, they are frequently perceived as characteristic reactions to pain, discomfort, fear, or perplexity.

Maladaptive mannerism can make one very unfriendly and unpopular with peers and superiors. One suffering from this issue will be radical and forthright in their attitude and conduct, and if they are not handled early enough, they can affect their ability to concentrate on things. Maladaptive mannerism nearly always indicates a need for help—real, qualified help—but it could go unnoticed until something severe happens.

With reference to Torey Hayden's book *One Child*, the idea of maladaptive behaviour, its various subcategories, and the mental health illnesses that can be associated with its use are discussed.

In *One Child*, Shelia's 18-year-old mother had abandoned her on the side of a highway two years before she had started attending classes. Sheila lives in an unhygienic one-room cabin with her violent, drunken father. She only has a pair of clothes and no access to water, so it is very obvious that she smells horrible. The other students in the class; also has their own problems to deal with and it is not surprising that they respond disapprovingly to her appearance on the first day of class. Sheila is very reserved and denies talking to any one or even gets up from her seat. She leaves her seat during lunch break only to gouge the eyes of the gold fish which adorned the class with the tip of a pencil. She runs away to the gym when she is discovered, and Hayden's had to gently pacify and get her back to the classroom. Sheila eventually starts trusting Hayden as a result of her continued patience and composure with her while she disobeys.

Hayden's complex portrayal tells the reader about her endurance, kindness, and tolerance with Sheila. Hayden's unrelenting love subdues Sheila and she learns how to communicate, and the two even start to enjoy doing each other's hair. Slowly, Sheila starts to open up as Hayden realises that Sheila's intelligence is way ahead of her grade level. As the narrative progresses, the reader is also made aware of more and more distressing aspects of Sheila's personal life, such as the occasion when her uncle brutally abused her sexually and even went so far as to slash her vagina, leaving the poor young girl to bleed profusely.

It is very apparent that neglect or harm caused by lack of care from parents during the formative years of a child can have a terrible impact. In Sheila's life this could be the primary factor that had led to her maladaptivemannerism. Conditions such as hunger, poverty, unhygienic, unsafe living environments and parent's failure to provide necessary supervision in upbringing a child can all be defined as neglect, as a child before Sheila had turned six she had gone through all these forms of torture in a large measure.

Salient features of maladaptive mannerism exhibited by Sheila

Avoidance

This is one of the key characteristics we see in Sheila as well. People with maladaptive disorders frequently avoid threats or detach from difficulties that they should not be avoiding.

In the case of Sheila , we observe that from a very early age, due to the difficulties she had experienced, the kid appears to be quite hostile, and in an effort to avoid people and relationships, Sheila makes herself seem even more distant. She also starts to reject individuals before she can do so herself since she has experienced a lot of rejection. This avoidance of conduct includes failing to make eye contact during conversations, speaking too quietly or not at all, and never, ever questioning until absolutely necessary. Avoidance does not improve coping skills in the long run. Invitations stop coming in, anxiety levels rise, and isolation results.

"Deep down behind those hostile eyes was a very little girl who had already learned that life isn't much fun for anybody; and the best way to avoid further rejection was to make herself as objectionable as possible". (*One Child* p. 29)

Withdrawal

This is another significant symptom of maladaptive mannerism. These kids are shy and tend to retreat from society; they typically shun social interactions while their classmates are around. The causes of childhood social isolation might range from social anxiety to a need for solitude. A wide variety of unfavourable adjustment outcomes, from early infancy to adolescence, are concurrently and predictably at risk for children who are socially reclusive. They face socio-emotional challenges and go through bouts of depression, anxiety, lack of confidence etc.

The main character Sheila serves as an archetype. She is not emotionally or cognitively capable of even comprehending anything about the nature of sexual assault, therefore lives in constant fear, she becomes secretive rather than informing people about her torture at home. She is aloof and always withdrawn by nature. Due to her mother's abandonment Sheila loses the ability to trust anyone, she is very cautious when anyone approaches her and looks at them with an eye of suspicion. She isolates herself and finds solace and comfort in her own company without involving anybody else. She is also very careful by not revealing her emotions. She had made up her mind never to shed tears and acknowledge her weakness.

Passive-aggressiveness

By being passively aggressively, an individual conveys his or her unpleasant emotions in an indirect manner. Their genuine emotions are reflected through their mannerisms and actions. Such people tend to express unpleasant emotions rather than directly addressing them. When someone acts in a passive-aggressive manner, there is dis-connectivity between their words and actions. The notable features of passive-aggressive mannerism is resentment and resistance to other people's demands, particularly to those who are in positions of power ,procrastination, refusal to cooperate, and making mistakes on purpose. This attitude arises in response to requests from others because they believe that by being unfriendly, glum, or cynical would enable them not to be taken advantage of or undervalued often.

In *One Child* we come across Hayden struggling with Sheila during her initial days of attending class, engaging Sheila as her teacher was very hectic and demanding for Hayden. Shelia would not accept her place as a student in the classroom; hence her conduct was quite chaotic and unpredictable. Shelia went so far as to flee, act out, and even gouge the fish's eyes out in the classroom. Hayden was aware that it would be challenging to identify Sheila's internal source of suffering which was the cause of her passive aggressiveness.

Anger

Anger is a fundamental and significant aspect of human existence. It exists because it provides a worthwhile and significant advantage, just like any other emotion. However, it may become maladaptive when experienced too strongly, for too long; or when individuals act negatively as a result of it, just like any other emotion. Anger that motivates an individual to take positive action is beneficial. If one becomes frequently upset or has furious outbursts, it is useless. Anger out of control doesn't make things go away. It makes people uncomfortable and hinders productive communication. This would apply to children having temper tantrums. Most kids soon become aware that there are more effective approaches to get the intended outcome.

The six-year-old Sheila from *One Child*, whose life was filled with abuse and negligence, is an illustration of a child who behaves in tolerably because she is unable to behave normally like other children because of her abusive background. Sheila was always angry and frequently treated the other kids in a very unkind way. She had never received instructions in kindness, manners, or consideration for others. She smacked the individual hard enough to gain back her spot in line when they took it from her. She would grab a toy that she desired from another child, wrestle it from of the child's hands, and run away to safety with it, hissing viciously at anyone who attempted to take it. This had the inevitable effect of making other kids dislike her and not wanting to play with her. She was not genuinely aware of how to behave differently or be nice.

The part played by Hayden in reviving Sheila in *One Child*

Each and every individual learns things in a different and unique manner, and Hayden was determined to identify the teaching methods that best matched each problematic or mentally challenged child's learning preferences. She also gave them instructions on proper mannerisms and etiquette, as well as what was expected of them in settings like their classroom or over lunch. The students listened to her because they respected her as a teacher and a real-life role model. All the students in her class had their own problems to deal with, but with Hayden's incessant help and relentless dedication they managed to overcome their difficulties to an extent which was remarkable. The small group got along well more as a family rather than a class. All had their own quirks, but yet they all cooperated and worked through them. Hayden had the ability for dealing with these kinds of pupils and assisting them in realising their full potential. She also had a talent for assisting the families of these students. Everyone has a special calling, and Hayden's was unquestionably to help troubled kids who had been abandoned and given up on even by their own family.

The humanitarian nature of Hayden's character, unconditional love, unrelenting endurance demonstrated in *One Child* proves that every child may be reached no matter what the circumstances are as long as a matured and experienced adult like Hayden could extend a warm and affectionate hand . The kind-hearted instructor taught Sheila love, support, and the value of trust in a relationship. The unwavering teacher in Hayden gave Sheila hope. In the book, Hayden's extraordinary ability to work with Sheila and impart self-respect as well as social skills is described.

The altruistic traits of Hayden's character shows how any child who hails from abusive environments both sexually and mentally may benefit through the loving kindness of an adult. Sheila learned about love, support, and the importance of trust from the kind-hearted teacher. The determined teacher gave Sheila reason to have hope. Hayden's amazing capacity to teach Sheila social skills and disseminate self-respect is recounted in this remarkable book.

This book *One Child* stands as a superb example delivered by a teacher called Hayden who was genuinely empathetic and kind. Reading the book made it clear that Hayden cared much about troubled children with emotional problems as well as slow learners. She was able to discern the brilliance and spark that Sheila was hiding underneath her rebellious and aggressive persona. Hayden began to view Sheila as a six-year-old child who had gone through difficult circumstances in life rather than as a troublemaker. Hayden gains Sheila's trust and becomes friendly with her, and the youngster experiences unimaginable transformations as a result. This life narrative, which modifies the viewpoint on the challenges of special education, melting the preconceptions that educators often believe special educators are proving to be accurate.

The book mentions Sheila as being a gifted youngster and scored really well on IQ tests and her intelligence was on par with those of the world's geniuses. But outsiders could only see the damage she had done and did not value her intelligence or the natural gifts that she possessed. Hayden spoke out and started to develop it. There was a terribly wounded and a violent person hiding under that little shell which Hayden understood. She started dealing in ways that made Sheila gain her confidence that Hayden would not betray her like her own mother and will not punish her like her father. This makes the child win Hayden's trust and open up gradually.

Each of her writings reflects the beneficial effects of teacher –student relationship. Hayden meets Sheila after seven years and narrates her experiences in the sequel titled *The Tiger's Child*. In the prologue of this book she mentions that, "This little girl had a profound effect on me. Her courage, her resilience, and her inadvertent ability to express that great gaping need to be loved that we all feel – in short "her humanness brought me into contact with my own." (The Tiger's Child p.8). The passionate testimonies in Hayden's books demonstrate that sharing one's life and love with those who reciprocate it is the most nourishing and healthy emotional experience imaginable.

Sheila had a big impact on me, as Hayden describes her in the opening to Tiger Child. Her bravery, her fortitude, and her unintentional capacity to articulate the immense, gaping desire for love that we all experience may be summed up as follows: "Her humanity brought me into contact with my own." (p.8) The passionate testimonies in Hayden's books demonstrate that sharing one's life and expressing love with those who reciprocate it is the most nourishing and healthy emotional experience imaginable.

Hayden followed some characteristic features or ideas that can be used as rules for interacting with children that are relationship-resistant. These qualities are reflected in Hayden's way of dealing with children who hail from troubled backgrounds, despite the fact that she avoids using any formal model or set procedures for developing relationships.

Exhibiting Love

Hayden exemplifies the affection shared between two individuals as a process of giving and nourishing someone rather than an emotion. Hayden offers herself whole heartedly when she discerns that it can cause change in a person. She is altruistic while sharing her curiosity, joy, understanding, wisdom, comedy, and melancholy, it enhances her children's lives and she receives her reward in the form of very small by gradual changes in their lives. Sheila stands as a typical example. Whenever Hayden addresses Sheila she uses terms like 'hon, Kitten etc' which has a great impact on the child, further she gives her simple gifts which are very precious to Sheila as she had never had any good things in life.

"She fingered the clips carefully through the plastic wrapping. With a frown she regarded me

"How come you do this?"

"Do what?"

"Be nice to me?"

I looked at her in disbelief. "Because I like you."

"Why? I be a crazy kid. I hurt your fishes. Why do you be nice to me?" (One Child p:87)

Also on several occasions in spite of Sheila being so dirty, Hayden hugs her makes her sit on her lap which has a great impact on Sheila as has never experienced such kind of love and affection from her parents nor anybody in her life. Hayden also proves through Sheila's example that loving the unlovable can transform one's life.

Effective Class Management

Hayden manages the most of the issues related to mannerism in her class with elegance and tact, making the utmost use of the opportunities to teach, establish trust, and promote relationship development in a very particular way. Hayden is shown as a teacher who relies on managing behaviour without using punishments and changing teaching strategies. She adopts a method of classroom management that emphasises warm interactions, making her pupils feel important and in charge as a consequence of the self

–importance they gain. Hayden does not set any hard and fast rules for her students. Hayden does not place a strong emphasis on the power, or good or negative repercussions initiated by the teacher, in influencing pupils' conduct. On the other hand, she concentrates her energies on outlining structure and ideals and requiring responsible, adult conduct.

Prevention

Prevention is one of the techniques Hayden uses which helps Sheila by not hurting herself as well as others in most of the occasions. She is very careful not to leave her alone without an adult' aid, also Hayden behaves cautiously in ways that will not provoke Sheila nor punishes her. She also proves as an embodiment of patience and endurance which at times is very astonishing and surprises Sheila for her misconduct.

Dedication

Dedication is another core factor that Hayden portrays, she selflessly dedicates her time and energy for her students she loved. She offers unwavering assistance when her students' needed it. This particular consideration and care benefits Sheila in particular, whether it be in terms of physical, mental, material, or emotional assistance. She goes out of the way to the migrant camp to meet Sheila's father. In order to meet each student's unique requirements, Hayden is able to put aside her own demands and even the institutional priorities such as their rules and regulations. In the case of Sheila she fights for her cause as she did not want the child to be committed to the hospital, she goes to an extent of seeking legal support to fight so that Sheila will have a normal life like any other child rather than being treated as a mentally imbalanced kid in a hospital.

Conclusion

Hayden has beautifully represented how she had established relationships with children on whom hope was lost. According to her teaching is not just the role of a teacher whereas establishing loving relationships mattered a lot , along with education, she also inculcates moral values and mannerisms which is mandatory for the growth of one's individual self. She is a teaching legend with invaluable resources who stands as an example that good understanding, patient dealing, and unconditional love will always have an impact on children. One never knows the background of a child which leads to maladaptive mannerism, but the intervention of a brilliant teacher can always have an optimistic change on child.

References

- One Child
- The Tiger's child
- https://cyc-net.org/cyc-online/cycol-0507-marlowe.html
- https://www.healthline.com/health/maladaptive-behavior
- file:///C:/Users/Staff/Downloads/Dialnet-FoundationsOfToreyHaydensRelationshipDriven
- Classro-216196%20(1).pdf.
- https://www.torey-hayden.com/research/1-final-pedagogy-caring.pdf.

Dr. Pauline V. N., works as an Assistant Professor in the Department of English, Kristu Jayanti College (Autonomous), Bengaluru. She has 12 years of teaching experience. Her areas of interests are Diasporic Writing, Post –Colonial Literature and Feminism.

Daffline Gladson, is a student of MSC Clinical Psychology (IYear) in Kristu Jayanti College (Autonomous), Bengaluru. Her areas of interests are Psychological Disorders and Feminism.

• • •

Inclusion of Theatre as a Pedagogical Tool in Rural Schools

Dr. Pavithra

Assistant Professor and Coordinator, Department of the Performing Arts, Kristu Jayanti College Autonomous and Cultural Coordinator of Bengaluru North University

Abstract

From ancient times to the present, the theatre has made contributions to the fields of education and numerous studies. The growth of theatre and how audiences view performances have both been impacted by the ongoing changes in the social, economic, political, and cultural landscape of humanity. Even the educational field has benefited from theatre as a cultural study. Several academics and sociocultural theorists have attempted to integrate theatre as a value system into education. The current worldwide environment has significantly altered the scope of theatre and its capacity to impart knowledge to students and people with a wide range of skills. The paper focuses on teaching through theatre and tries to explore theatre as a major pedagogical tool in the teaching school curriculum by teachers in the rural sector. The paper will be of great importance, especially in the context of post-colonial and globalized India.

Keywords: Pedagogy, Rural Schools, Theatre, Education, Curriculum

Introduction and Implications:

Drama courses, drama teachers, and theatre are included in the activity schedule at 60% of private kindergartens and some private elementary schools in Karnataka. These activities include puppetry, storytelling, music, painting, mask-wearing, and other topics. On request, the organization for modern theatre provides in-service training to kindergartens, and elementary and secondary schools in an effort to serve as a central authority for the training of new instructors.

The Department of State Education Research and Training (DESERT), which routinely offers seminars for teachers, provides academic leadership in rural school education and seeks to raise the standard of instruction in rural primary and secondary schools throughout the State. Pre-service teachers at the university are enrolled in theatre training courses organized by the Ministry of Education.

In Karnataka, 60% of private kindergartens and certain private elementary schools offer drama classes, have drama teachers on staff, and include theatre in their activity programs that cover topics like puppetry, storytelling, music, painting, mask-wearing, and other related topics. The Association for modern theatre aims to serve as a central authority for teacher preparation and provides in-service training to kindergartens, elementary schools, and high schools upon request.

The National Council of Educational Research and Training (NCERT) has included education through theatre as one of the techniques it strongly advocated, and NGOs have been asked to promote these recommendations.

The theatre has been employed as a development tool by many organizations and initiatives for a variety of purposes, including teaching, propaganda, rehabilitation, participation, and development exploration.

The development of theatre in education has recently benefited from the efforts of numerous theatre groups and organizations.

The National Bal Bhavan, Navodaya Vidyalayas, National School of Drama, Centre for Cultural Resources and Training, National Museums, Sangeeth Natak Academy, Indian Mime Theatre, Indian Foundation for the Art, Sutradhar, Ninasam, and other organizations have all been actively working in the field of theatre and education, encouraging aspiring academics to pursue research. These groups have produced cadres of knowledgeable fans, disseminated information about dramatic literature, and organized theatre events that involved numerous students.

As William Shakespeare quotes, "The play is the thing, but the power and the promise of the theatre education lie not only in students observing drama on the stage and screen but also in their own theatre in the classroom." Students may see and witness a variety of plays on stage and in movies, but the whole experience of watching and acting, which is equally vital, is provided by the theatre in the classroom.

As Albert Einstein quotes "Imagination is more important than knowledge" That is what makes theatre, particularly for the young, potentially the most powerful educational experience. It achieves all these through a construct that is completely imagined. Without imagination, education is a kind of intellectual recycling of the same knowledge passed from teacher to student and back to the teacher during tests.

The work or service has not yet reached many rural schools, despite the fact that a lot of programmes in this region are operating successfully. The majority of the urban and rural schools included in the research study demonstrate that more than 70% of schools lack adequate curriculum guides, teaching materials, government-funded teacher training, assistance for theatrical professionals, class time, and other things. Without these supplies, it is challenging for schools, particularly those in remote areas, to start or maintain theatre programmes.

Problem Statements:

In our state of Karnataka, 13,800 government schools with fewer than 25 students are on the verge of closing. All of these schools are located in rural areas, and approximately 1,800 of them have fewer than ten students. The plan to upgrade one school in every hobli into a "model school" has raised questions, despite the fact that the Department of school education and Literacy asserts that there is no possibility of closure. Experts say that in the name of a merger, the department will move students from low-admission schools to model schools. Students would be enticed and encouraged to attend these schools if theatre practitioners continuously experimented with theatre elements to bring about a qualitative change at this time.

The research was conducted with an experimental design that rural students have shown improvement both subject-wise as well as overall personality development using theatre as a method to learn. Even the teachers analyzed the process of teaching as productive. But the teachers felt that they lack the knowledge resource of theatre and the resource available in their teaching process environment.

From the data/information collected through descriptive and qualitative vs quantitative research design, it is found that teachers from many rural and semi-rural schools accepted the process of teaching the curriculum using theatre as a medium. But once asked about the implementation of this process their response suggested that they lack theatre knowledge and resources. This led to the analysis and finding that a policy or syllabus should be implemented in the curriculum in teacher training (D.Ed., B.Ed., M.Ed.), or related teaching sector.

The paper tries to examine the potential for educational knowledge through theatre while collecting ethnographic and empirical data using this conceptual layer.

In the process of studying or teaching through theatre, the majority of our understandings and learning will always be pushed to the limit and collide with one another. Scenic design will allow the learner to become creatively engaged in the learning process since it contrasts most physical displays of content. This paper which is focused on theatre and education tries to explore theatre as a major pedagogical tool in teaching rural students school curriculum. The paper will surely be of great importance, especially in the context of post-colonial and globalized India.

The table shows Rural school teachers' opinions on theatre education.

Sl. No.	Views on Theatre Education	Highly Agree		Agree		Disagree		Highly Disagree		No Comment	
		F	%	F	%	F	%	F	%	F	%
1.	Theatre enhances aesthetic development	33	33.0	66	66.0	1	1.0	-	-	-	-
2.	Theatre is an Effective teaching method	38	38.0	61	61.0	-	-	-	-	1	1.0

Source: Field Research

Theatre is an Effective teaching method in Rural Schools

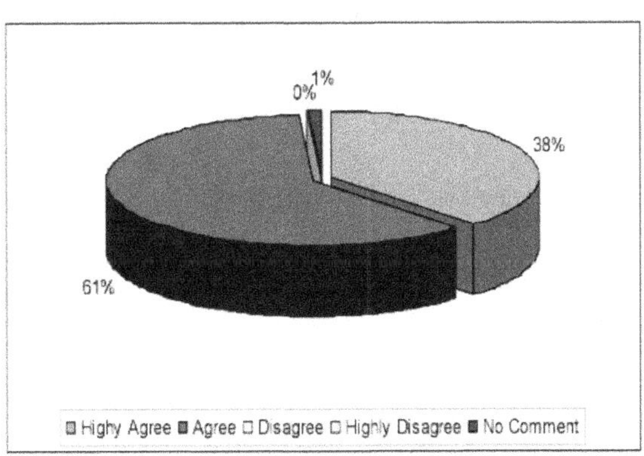

According to the above table, 33% of the teachers strongly concur that theatre fosters artistic development. 66% of respondents agree, while 1% disagree. Theatre is an effective educational tool, according to 38% and 66% of respondents, with 1% remaining uncommented. Overall, 98% of educators concur that theatre is an excellent teaching strategy that may be used to successfully improve students' aesthetic sensibilities in rural schools.

The above table's general conclusion is that more than 95% of instructors in rural schools agree that theatre fosters aesthetic development and serves as a useful teaching strategy in these settings.

Objectives of Introducing Theatre in Pedagogy:

- To promote theatre as a successful educational tool in remote areas
- To develop theatre as an ethnic-educative technique that opens doors for collaboration with rural teacher communities. To collaborate with B.Ed, D.Ed, M.Ed, and rural teachers on theatre approaches and their applications to the educational process.
- Giving these teachers in remote areas a place or sphere where they can experiment with the students and explore issues and opportunities while instructing using theatrical tactics.
- Examining the drawbacks of the conventional, mainstream teaching approach.
- To investigate theatre as a teaching tool in the Indian context, with a particular focus on female instructors.
- Provide an innovative curriculum that supports multidisciplinary instruction.
- Theater education should be provided for rural school teachers.

The theater may be a significant and helpful resource at a time when educators around the nation are experimenting with new approaches to inspire rural students so they will stay in school and continue, as well as innovative approaches to prepare a whole new generation for life in a quickly changing world.

Significant amounts of research are not conducted from the standpoint of theatre, particularly from the performative perspective of theatre in the rural context.

Another significant aspect is that it makes an effort to examine theatre history from an educational perspective, particularly in the context of rural education. Due to the historical marginalization of educational theatre, this will help us better comprehend theatre.

Conclusion:

In the urban sector, theatre education is a well-liked medium. However, if this medium is used in our rural sector, which has a richer culture than the rapidly changing city, it will have a positive impact on education.

Numerous educators have worked to improve education because it is one of the factors that trainees' quality of life. children according to grade level and have turned education into a one-sided process. In order to identify, motivate, and meet the various requirements of pupils in the rural sector, a new method or strategy is required.

Theatrical education offers these pupils a genuine alternative to traditional classroom instruction. It is one sort of entertainment that has no end and keeps developing forever. Working with rural, urban, preschool, special needs, or poor children doesn't limit one's ability to capture their imagination and creative enthusiasm. Hence, theatre pedagogy in rural schools needs to be supported and promoted by everyone. So, it is important for everyone to support and promote theatre education in rural schools.

References

- Kothari C. R, "Research Methodology, Methods and Techniques." New Age International Publishers, 2009.
- Kim Alan Wheetley, "The Promise of the Theatre Education." South East Centre for the Arts, 2012.
- Jerome S Bruner, "Play: its role and development and evolution." Penguin Publisher, 1976

- "Art Education in India" Country Report, Department of Education in Arts & Aesthetics National Council of Educational Research & Training Ministry of Human Resource Development - Govt. of India,2010.
- Baldwin P and Fleming K, "Teaching Literacy through Drama." New York, Routledge Falmer, 2003, pg: 4
- Alain and Becham , "Theatre" , 4th Edition-, Cambridge Publication, 2008

Dr Pavithra, is working as an Assistant Professor and Coordinator, Department of the Performing Arts, Kristu Jayanti College Autonomous and Cultural Coordinator of Bengaluru North University. She is part of the Board of Studies and Board of Examination at various universities across India. She is a Kannada Theatre artist and Actress and has also performed Kannada play at Feltham, London, UK. Moreover, she has also received the National award - Theatre Academician Award 2022 for excellence in teaching theatre for more than a decade by Ministry of Culture, Government of India.

• • •

CHAPTER XI

Engendered City Spaces: Functional Marginalities

Dr. Sreedevi Santhosh

Assiatant Professor, Department of English, Kristu Jayanti College (Autonomous), Bengaluru

Abstract

Landscape design is rooted in hegemonic power, cities conceived by scientists, planners and urbanists view human relationships through its lens, goal and orientation aimed at homogeneity. This design discounts in the process 'lived' experiences of women, other underprivileged social groups and minorities. With this notion as backdrop the paper attempts to explore if experiences of space, in the city of Bangalore, transformed by technological advances, its metros, sky scrapers, road rush, collaborative work spaces...bring together residual, dominant and emergent elements of cultural production in unimagined ways. The paper explores whether Bengaluru's shift into Bangalore through its cosmopolitan facelift has been better inclusive of the considered categories and if its perception as an exclusively male space has changed. Inquiring into what experiences, institutional norms and social relations bring about this change, the study is an attempt to mark 'self –construction' in relation to the changing city, evaluating opportunities subject to mobility with its transformation into a hyper-urbanised space, marked by its sky scrapers, metros, ola and uber, swiggy and zomato, media of transit and to explore if it tangentially transforms into zones of safety or if it cramps individuation.

Keywords: City design, Marginalities, Cosmopolitanism

Travelling the city is a prototype of an individual's relationship with their conditions of existence. In public places the 'phatic', seemingly random every day encounters, snippets of conversations with co-travellers or strangers are coded. The 'haptic': the sense of touch, sound, sight and smell that initiates bodily encounters driving this field of human interactions: separates, purifies, demarcates, punishes transgression, systematising experiences. Metro cabins allotted exclusively for women is for instance a code that allows one to read engendered 'phatic' encounters as disruptive almost always violent depending on whether the trains are in transit or at halt, the perpetrator slips out menacingly, the affected moves on, unattended with no immediate redressal mechanisms at work, with his/her sense of being violated drowning in the noise of propaganda, advertisements, hate speech and fake news. Perec in what is considered a 'thought experiment' attempts to "see what happens when nothing happens"(Perec (2010) by spending three days monitoring a street in Paris recording the 'everyday', not considered worthy of attention. The public sphere shaped supposedly by random, abrupt encounters is in reality a potent field of political human interrelationships. The act of narrating it becomes a social contract between the writer and the public, holding possibilities of 'writing' wrongs, additions and revisions of policies in the interest of human rights.

But given that we live in times with the "paradox of simultaneity, shortage and excess" (Appadurai), "shrunk and expanded" all at once, human beings are under siege with the pandemic, surgically reshaped, surviving on packaged food, malnutrition, dangerous conditions of work and horrendous forms of sanitary infrastructure making bodies vulnerable. Human beings put up with "inconceivable levels of atmospheric pollutants, invisible forms of digital radiation from new tech devices, dangerous fantasies around the body, enhanced forms of fake vitality and energy ranging from viagra to cocaine, constantly persuaded to think that we are on the edge of various tech utopias promised by the internet of things by biometric identification systems, robotics, artificial intelligence and virtual technology". (Appadurai)

The body being our interface with this world, embodiment its attempt to participate and rewire anticipating risks, the list of encounters in this world of technological reproduction seemingly endless, the body's attempt to mediate these risks may be futile. It is through conspicuously drawing out differences between 'within and without', 'above and below', 'male and female', 'with and against' that a semblance of order is created. , identities are constructed and reconfigured forever in a state of flux with the body's encounters with other bodies, shaping and reshaping itself. Lynching on MG Road and Brigade road on new year's eve for instance met with demonstrations led by students swarming the streets, flagging slogans, 'I will go out', "My body, my right", "I will not be told where I cannot go", "I want to be heard when I talk about this, people must listen", "The shame belongs to the person who commits the crime, not the woman". "It is not about being safe - it is about being free..." Drawing on India's History of witch hunting Nayar writes that the process of "apportioning blame is a purificatory ritual...an identified person is invested with all evils of that culture" Nayar (2009). Its interpretation that materialise as injunctions around sartorial code, time –place curfews is exhausting. The Culture and Tourism Minister's advisory to foreign women to not wear skirts to avoid violence may at face value seem like an act of caution but the interpretation of violence that is afflicted on women or the lesser privileged is 'saturating' rooted in misogyny, commodification of the body and stereotypical notions that are circulated on who counts and don't. Working on principles of exclusion and eviction this 'group sentiment' draws on already circulating ideas and ways of thinking justified on grounds that one ought not be around on Brigade road at that point in time, at midnight, to rather be caught in the privacy of their homes instead of being 'on the move' , These responses are mere deductions of an impending crisis into loose morality standards taking attention off the issue to focus on a larger culturally sanctioned telling of 'morality'. This inability to pin things down into specificities has to largely do with the condition of being in 'flow', signifying 'connected' worlds mobile with ideas, goods, news , money or sentiments, all of which create a semblance of reality sacrificing emphatic comforts of the 'everyday'. "Small communications of 'gaze', 'touch', 'words', 'the murmurs of the social without a lexicon that make up the living tissues of a social world" (Appadurai)

Public transport is uninhabitable with violence, assault, stalking, ogling, public impunity/ apathy towards sexualised violence has a lot to do with haptic technologies becoming delayed in genuine human contact or communication that transpires in megabytes at present. Infrastructural designs, Metro stations / roads / Boarding points are coded as 'masculine' that exclude the undocumented, refugee, the LGBT community, because of the heightened sense of profundity that it alone can validate. City planners do not account for its demographic that is 'unstable', 'shifting', 'uncertain' and, above all 'contested'.

'New shoots in Old roots', Chiranjiv Singh's *The Cultural Backdrop of Bangalore* in Adithi De's *Multiple Cities* opens with the line "we were simple people, these north Indians have come and spoilt us". De (2008) Heterogeneous in linguistic, cultural and physical terms the city of Bangalore retains if only scathingly, it's colonial and Anglo-Indian pasts, the least in terms of labels namely the 'cantonment'. Bangalore's co-existence with Bengaluru at its best, suggests this bewilderment or perplexity in the absence of its traditional sign posts. Is Bengaluru's transformation into Bangalore in the last two decades weaned through the 'cultural logic of late capitalism' emulating as the world does, 'Globalisation'? Do experiences of space being transformed by technological advances, with its metros, sky scrapers, road rush, collaborative work spaces, bring together residual, dominant and emergent elements of cultural production in hitherto unimagined ways? Feminist philosophy draws attention to the evident silencing of women, the marginalisation of experiences and its lack of expression in discourses of the post liberal fragmented world making claims for redressal of their identities through 'degendering' urban design.

The cosmopolitan image that binds people to Bangalore makes it an eclectic space. Bangalore today is considered a city without a fixed image, like how De narrates it "a city of myriad tongues", "multiple origins", "cacophony of soundtracks" with "curvilinear recounting" , its "glocal spirit" (De 2008). De maintains that Bangalore "is a continuum where the past, present and future collide every milli-moment jeans pants in the outside, madi panche in the inside" (De 2008). Bangalore according to De retells hidden stories in whispers, narratives 'thread bare' yet 'convergent'. Bangalore being a favoured location for Information Technology and Business Process Outsourcing companies, the city's impending growth is outstripped with globalisation.

In the city, 'take-away' phenomenon, 'food for the road', 'on the road' reconfigures its consumption pattern. Inequities work around this 'non place' delivery outlet delocalised from everything. "Food mobilities affect connections between home and away" Nayar(2009), the delivery 'boy' being on the move and the outlet, the food provider, the' human' is camouflaged/ dislodged. The instance of service providers relenting on delivery time, the news report sounding techie cancels food order consequently the delivery boy punches her, suggest delay in meaningful 'phatic' interactions. Technology is an alibi for ambivalence, allowing access on the one hand, problematizing it on the other, narratives 'flowing' in this paradox of access and trouble. City planning impacts movement in the city, the consumer's relationship with the delivery boy, with the man in transit, also changed the way the city functioned. Not so far off conversations around how zomato delivery boys ate up a share of what they had to deliver is only too close to how there is a need to redesign the layout of roads dug up and down to make way for metros. Tech histories of co –work spaces, café's , collaborative work spaces, studios for living / startups in cities , mark human relationships within a social field that gives the city its face lift alternately opening up newer readings of class privilege , gender politics , new forms of vagrancies (survival in transit , 'dun so' boys , zomato , swiggy delivery boys, migrants and refuges

Techno advances like accessing apps as means of sustenance and tracking movement are intertwined on the one hand with problems that come with access manipulated as tracking / surveillance mechanisms. The access that swiggy has for instance to one's tastes blurs so much of what is private into the public sphere. Safety apps that came out after the Nirbhaya incident mostly do not work, with guardian /patronising attitudes that become surveillance mechanisms. This understanding of the city shapes consciousness, artists stand -up comedians create subversive responses that reconfigure the city in unimagined ways, the graffiti work of the transgender, writing out city spaces as there's is an attempt at narrating the city in their own terms. Young adults talked about how moments of transit are most vulnerable, in metro cabins for instance as creeps and cranks slip in and out stealthily. Bangalore today is for them a place susceptible to more of violence, a 'herd mentality' of sorts with growing access to the internet.

Drawing on Marx's notion that the "real and the not-real are constantly cross-referenced in the productive activity by which humans interact with the world, changing the not-real allows one to think differently about the real, its possibilities and its actualities" Miéville (2002). I would like to argue for a need to 'degender' design for bodies to act within, including those that do not matter, the 'not-real' within spaces. The body is inscribed with spatial markers, places are configured by hegemonic interrelationships that write and rewire the body anticipating 'risks' but the 'staticity' in urban design construes the validation of variety in demographic inflow . New forms of urban development create high-end, exclusive zones of consumerism and residential layouts. that cannot be redesigned with the rapidity with which encounters in the world reassign us "Those who engineer hyper-surveilled urban environments justify them not only in terms of general public safety but in terms of risk management, arguing that such environments enact a form of preventative policing that reduces risk and obviates the need for 'reactive' policing. Beyond surveillance cameras, this ideology is literally built into the urban spatial environment in the form of building sight lines, restricted passageways, closed public toilets, and other forms of CPTED – 'crime prevention through environmental design." (Ross 2016)

Homogeneity in city designs do not validate those categories that are not inscribed as culturally marked, the undocumented , sexual minorities also those pedestrians who largely pass as not value assigned 'to walk is to lack space'(Tally). 'Rights' for all of these categories marked with the metaphor of movement is precarious. These in transit identities are configured with invisibility. With gender identities and spaces changing with socialisation, there is an inimitable need to 'degender' urban design.

References

- Appaurai, Arjun. (2021, Feb 9). Globalisation and New Terrains of consciousness: phenomenologies of the Global/local/ https://youtu.be/vAvLUKL9Uo0
- De, Adithi. (2008). Multiple cities: Writings on Bangalore. Penguin books.
- Nayar, Pramod, K. (2009). Packaging Life: Cultures of everyday. SAGE Publications India Pvt Ltd.
- Perec, Georges. , Lowenthal, Marc. , (Trans). (2010). An Attempt at Exhausting a Place in Paris. Wakefiled Press, Reprint.
- Ross, Ian, Jeffrey. (2016). Routledge Handbook of Graffiti and Street Art. New York, Routledge.

Dr. Sreedevi Santhosh, has been teaching English Studies and Cultural Studies for the last 15 years. Areas of interest Spatiality , Gender Studies and Regional Studies. She is an Assistant Professor at the Department of English, Kristu Jayanti Collge, Bengaluru.

CHAPTER XII

The Deception of Inclusivity: Challenging the Paradigm of 'Community' in Cults Like 'Children of God' and 'Scientology'

Josephine Mercy

Assistant Professor, Women's Christian College, Chennai

Abstract

Cults have been long been known as groups that strip off people's identities and leave them with a sense of hopelessness right at its outset. In reality, cults, like any abusive relationship says experts, start with the cult leaders showering immense love and admiration on the people who decide to be a part of these groups. Jim Jones' 'The Peoples Temple' and Charles Manson's 'The Manson Family' are some examples of how cults grow in popularity due to their ability to win over crowds by preaching about comradeship and instilling a sense of being a part of a community that willingly accepts people, without any questions. The want of being a part of something or feeling desired after has been identified as the factor that pushes people to fall willingly into these cults. 'Children of God' and 'Scientology' are cult groups that have secured the hearts of millions across the globe owing to their powerful philosophies, which on thorough investigation, prove to be rooted on sham and trickery. The idea of inclusivity and the feeling of superiority that comes with being insiders to these groups are still attracting young and old alike to join these destructive forces. This paper attempts to study the paradigm of community that is built in these cults and the redeeming power of education that has freed the minds of people from falling deeper into these abysses of chaos. It also tries to emphasise that not all communities that promise inclusion provide it in its truest sense.

Keywords: Cults, inclusivity, insiders, community, education.

The post-modern world has been plagued by wars, nuclear weapons, trauma, violence and sicknesses. On one hand, the rise of ecoterrorism has been proven to be detrimental to nature and on the other hand, human beings have themselves brought forth much disaster through deceit to ensure their well-being.

One such forms of manipulation that is growing rapidly in the modern world is the upsurge of cults. Cults are of different kinds and they come in all sizes. As the well renowned cult critic and clinical psychologist Margaret Thaler Singer said, "Cults are truly personality cults. Because cult structure is basically authoritarian, the personality of the leader is all important" (XXIV).

The success of a cult is largely dependent on the cult leader. These leaders are self-appointed and recruit people. He/she is often seen as a charismatic person and exercises complete authority over the group. The founder of 'Children of God' (COG), David Berg, strongly believed that sex is a gift from God and that the best way to use this gift is by exploring it with whoever and whenever needed or possible. The group had often been accused of sexual misconduct, rape, theft and unfair treatment of its followers.

Scientology was founded by Lafayette Ronald Hubbard who was chiefly popular as an American author of science fiction books. Scientology was started as a way to help people find themselves and be relieved of the trauma that affect their lives. The cult has been accused by the Cult Awareness Network of being "the most ruthless, the most classically terroristic, the most litigious and the most lucrative cult the country has ever seen" (Healy 58).

The primary aim of cults is to create a utopia for the leader and the followers. Though not all cults are religious, the cult leaders are most often treated with utmost reverence and worshipped as gods. The cult leaders entice their followers with such promises of a better future and prosperous life. The only way to experience the fulfilment of this promise, according to the norms of these groups, is by surrendering one's critical mind and put his/her trust in the leader with a heart full of faith. Questions of any kind are not only discouraged but are also considered to be intolerable.

Singer had identified the main reasons why people join radical cults. Vulnerable and depressed people are most often the targets. It is important to note that many people who are a part of cults are educated and highly successful in their careers. It is hence undeniable that cult leaders work strategically and use many different methods to lure people into their groups.

One such important factor that attracts people to join cults is the promise of relationships and a community. 'Children of God' worked on the principle that sex is not exclusive to couples. It was seen as a free gift that can be 'enjoyed' by anyone. Young girls, in the name of honouring God, were subject to rape and abuse to please the men around them. Their groups comprised of many men and women who lived together and devoted themselves to serving the vision of their founder. Just like many cults, Berg had forbidden any kind of literature inside his community. His followers were expected to read and re-read his ideologies that were printed in the regular newsletter which was titled as Mo Letters. The publication included his goals for the community, explicit sexual cartoon drawings and a portion was dedicated to slander those who left the group.

This type of extreme subjugation is possible only after months and even years of brainwashing. It is what Singer calls as "invisible social adaptation" (61). People are put through what psychologists term as thought reform process. This is achieved primarily through by controlling the person's social/physical environment. One of the main reasons why most cults usually force their followers to live together is because of the clash that happens between their beliefs and the outside world.

Unlike COG, Peoples Temple and Manson's Family, Scientology never forces its people in settle in their quarters. Singer points out that manipulation can happen effectively even when people go to work every day. They are expected to do activities that are cult-related in their free time.

Members of Scientology go through a process called 'auditing' to search for the sources of their trauma and eventually work to attain the state of 'clear'. The group emphasises on the importance of mental health and promises to serve humankind but prices its 'services' at an exorbitant fee. Similar to the Mo Letters, Hubbard's book on cosmology and mental health has become the group's sacred scripture.

Recruits are usually brought to workshops, camps or weekend retreats to isolate them from access to their usual social groups. "When cut off from social support, social background, families, familiar surroundings, friends, jobs, schoolmates, and classes and brought into new environs with a new ambience, few can resist the pull to fit in" (Singer 114).

Cult members are slowly made to avoid reflective and critical thinking and engage themselves with working towards spreading the vision of their cult leader. COG's followers were expected to go on the mission called "Flirty Fishing" where women would lure men to their group by freely involving in sexual activities. Faith Jones, the granddaughter of David Berg, records in her book Sex Cult Nun how her mother and a few other women disdained the project but would do it to honour God and serve their leader.

Scientology is well-known because it is a group that boasts of having celebrities and rich people as its members. Some decide to terminate their membership after taking a few courses while a select few dedicate their lives to this 'church' entirely that they decide to stay in the Scientology property. Scientologists have been known to talk about their joyful experiences to the outsiders and help them get a glimpse of the privileges of being a part of the church. The followers of COG, likewise, would go out and attempt to recruit new followers through "Flirty Fishing" and other means.

They talk about "how members had left lives of travail and now led lives of joy, camaraderie, and blessedness and that ended with urging the listener to come with the members into this happy family" (Singer 165).

The testimonies of torture, acts of paedophilia and insensitive treatment of human beings are hidden from plain sight. The insider status that the cult receives is portrayed as something that is worthy to be coveted for. The newcomers usually learn from the others that "the more hideously they portrayed their pasts, the more approval the leader gave" (Singer 165). Every member feels the pressure of pleasing his/her leader to enjoy special privileges.

Similar to Scientology, there are many cult groups that offer nonprofessional therapy. Singer talks of an experienced clinician who was a member of a group for many years. The clinician, blinded by her devotion to the group, was oblivious to the fact that she was under the hands of an expert manipulator, despite being trained to find one. "Somehow when I was around him, I lost my sense of self. I lost all my knowledge, all my diagnostic skills. I failed to recognise a brilliant psychopath had control over me" (Singer 180).

Many ex-Scientologists and ex-COG members have given various reasons as to why they could not leave these groups a lot sooner. Singer categorises these into what she calls as the five D's.
1. Deception
2. Debilitation
3. Dependency
4. Dread
5. Desensitization (Singer 266).

Cults are rooted on deception. The members stay in the state of oblivion throughout their membership. Those who find out the group's dark secrets, constantly seek ways to escape after witnessing alarming things.

Ron Hubbard Sr., the founder of Scientology, was a man who was a hard-drinker and abused his family constantly. When his book Dianetics became an instant success, he opened a clinic to treat people to cure their sadness while all along his own wife and child were miserable in his own household. People thronged to his doorstep begging for help from a science-fiction writer. Hubbard was so convincing that they treated him as a doctor and put their entire trust in him. The members would go through various processes and kept within the safe walls of the church. The deception was successful also because of what Hubbard's son called as a "fair-game doctrine" ("Inside the Church of Scientology"). They would do all they can to stop journalists from inspecting the church. Jim Jones and his church were also reported to have prevented ongoing investigation and even murdered a few correspondents.

The next D according to Singer is Debilitation. Years of psychological persuasion and inner conflict prevent people from leaving the cult groups immediately after sensing danger. Faith Jones, David Berg's granddaughter, recalls how her mother had to see her husband marry another woman and still go with it as part of God's divine plan. The strife in her mind continued for many years to follow.

Dependency and Dread go hand-in-hand as strong strategies to keep people from leaving the group. Psychiatrist Robert Lifton identified eight psychological themes as central to a totalistic environment. The first theme is what he called as "Milieu control" (Singer 70). He highlights how members of a few cults are prevented from gossiping and reading so that they could constantly be fed with the doctrines of the groups they belong to. They end up depending on cults entirely that they dread leaving them as they know not of any other way of survival. Hubbard's son was recorded commenting thus: "All cults, including Scientology, say, "I am your mind, I am your brain. I've done all the work for you, I've laid the path open for you. All you have to do is turn your mind off and walk down the path I have created."" ("Inside the Church of Scientology").

The last D mentioned is Desensitization. People become numb to things that once bothered them because of years of mind-control and brainwashing.

Ronald Dewolf, the son of the founder of Scientology, was the church's director of training where he oversaw the training of thousands of people. He had designed the procedures and had observed closely the effect that this church had on people. Despite witnessing the overpriced fee that was collected from people and the money that was swindled, Hubbard Jr., became passive as he strongly believed in the procedures they set up for people. The breaking point happened when his father got involved with the Russians.

In Educated, Tara Westover recorded her experiences of escaping the fanatical views of Mormonism that her parents endorsed. They had made sure their children never went to school and prevented them from being exposed to the literature of the outside world. She went ahead to realise that life was much more than what her parents had opened up for her. Westover became open-minded by the power of education and was able to get her PhD from Trinity College, Cambridge. This led to her being ostracised by her family.

Faith Jones risked her life and went against the expectations of the group's codes to study to become a lawyer later in life. Both Jones and Westover realised the saving power of education after escaping the grasps of the dangerous cult groups they were part of.

Hubbard Jr., and other ex-Scientologists risked their lives when they fled from the group. They received several threats and were falsely accused. This multi-million-dollar business hires the best lawyers to defend its cases. Common man is left with no choice but to keep absolute silence about the intimidations. Above all, Scientology affects the mind and soul of a human being. In the pretence of making a huge impact on one's mind, the cult controls it. Hubbard Jr., attested to this statement when he said, "Scientology and all the other cults are one-dimensional, and we live in a three-dimensional world. Cults are as dangerous as drugs. They commit the highest crime: the rape of the soul" ("Inside the Church of Scientology").

Education redeems human beings from various bondages. Enlightenment, either through formal education or that which is gained through personal quest, is probably one of the very few ways that one can go to for the purpose of truly being free of such traps. True insight into these matters, it must be noted, is not always acquired by formal education. Netflix's documentary, Wild Wild Country, is proof that a charismatic leader can entrap intellectuals such as doctors, lawyers and teachers with his philosophies no matter how outlandish they might seem to outsiders.

Tara Westover's remarks about education may perhaps serve as the most fitting description of education by someone who truly appreciates it: "You could call... selfhood many things. Transformation. Metamorphosis. Falsity. Betrayal. I call it an education" (333).

References

- Healy, David. Let Them Eat Prozac: The Unhealthy Relationship between the Pharmaceutical Industry and Depression. New York U.P., 2006.
- "How Does Scientology Get Its Followers to Believe That the World Outside of the Gates Is so Horrible?" Quora, www.quora.com/How-does-Scientology-get-its-followers-to-believe-that-the-world-outside-of-the-gates-is-so-horrible.
- "Inside The Church of Scientology: An Exclusive Interview with L. Ron Hubbard, Jr." Penthouse, inside the Church of Scientology an Exclusive Interview with L Ron Hubbard Jr (Aka Ron DeWolfe), lermanet.org/scientologynews/penthouse-LRonHubbardJr-interview-1983.html.
- Singer, Margaret Thaler, and Robert Jay Lifton. Cults in Our Midst: The Continuing Fight Against Their Hidden Menace. Revised and Updated, Jossey-Bass, 2003.
- Westover, Tara. Educated. Random House, 2018. yes-pdf.com. https://yes- pdf.com/electronic-book/2722. PDF file.

Ms. Josephine Mercy, is an Assistant Professor in the PG Department of English at Women's Christian College, Chennai, India. Her areas of interest and research are Holocaust Studies, Cult Literature, British Literature and American Literature. She enjoys teaching British History, American Poetry, Literary Criticism and Theory, New Literatures and Research Methodology at both under and postgraduate levels. Ms Josephine has presented papers at national and international conferences and published research papers in various journals.

• • •

CHAPTER XIII

An Exclusive Inclusivity of All Sexual Minorities in Queer Theory: An Exclusive Analysis of Sarah Schulman's Select Novels

Joseph K. J.[1] and Dr. J Amalaveenus[2]

[1]Ph.D Research Scholar, St. Joseph's College (Autonomous), Affiliated to Bharathidasan University, Trichy, 620002, Tamil Nadu, India
[2]Assistant Professor of English, St. Joseph's College (Autonomous), Affiliated to Bharathidasan University, Trichy, 620002, Tamil Nadu, India

Abstract

This paper explores inclusivity of all sexual minorities in queer theory and the inadequacy and exclusivity of other theories and terms to be inclusive of all sexual orientations in the light of the select novels of queer novelist Sarah Schulman. The term patriarchy excluded the feminine gender. Feminism excluded the masculine gender. Gay/lesbian studies excluded all sexual orientations other than homosexuality. The Term LGBT included only Lesbians, Gays, Bisexuals, and Transgender and excluded all others. Here, queer theory appeared on the silver screen as a term that includes all sexual orientations. The term "queer" may be used by anybody who resists conforming to established social or sexual norms; this includes, probably, guys who identify as straight. This quote emphasises that the term queer theory is an inclusive term that includes all sexual orientations. Sarah Schulman, An American queer writer and activist, uses the term queer to refer to all sexual minorities in her works. Where exclusivity builds a wall amidst people, inclusivity builds a bridge where people can easily connect with all people irrespective of their sexual orientations. Let the use of the term queer cure the wounds created by exclusivity and care to build a world of peace made up of the attitude of inclusivity.

Key Words: Inclusivity, Exclusivity, Queer, Gay/lesbian studies, Feminism, Patriarchy

---

Introduction

This study examines the inclusion of all sexual minorities in queer theory, as well as the incompetence and exclusivity of other theories and concepts in terms of their ability to be inclusive of all sexual orientations, in light of the selected books written by the queer author Sarah Schulman. The concept of patriarchy did not include the female gender. The masculine gender was not included in feminism. Studies on gays and lesbians did not include participants from any sexual orientation other than homosexuality. The term LGBT did not encompass any additional sexual orientations or gender identities other than lesbians, gays, bisexuals, and transgender people. In the world of cinema, the phrase "queer theory" was first used to refer to a concept that included all types of sexual orientation. As Jackson and Jones state that anyone who feels at odds with the social or sexual convention can claim the label "queer", including, presumably, heterosexual men" (124). Presumably, it includes guys who identify as heterosexual too. This statement highlights the fact that the phrase "queer theory" is an inclusive term that includes all sexual orientations. Specifically, it emphasises the fact "queer theory". In her writings, the American author and activist Sarah Schulman, who identifies as queer, uses the word "queer" to refer to all forms of sexual minorities. Inclusiveness fosters an environment where people can readily interact with one another regardless of the sexual orientations of those around them. At the same time, exclusivity tends to construct barriers between individuals based on sexual inclinations. The usage of the word "queer" should serve as a salve for the wounds caused by exclusivity, and we should take care to construct a world of peace based on an attitude of inclusiveness.

Meaning of Exclusivity and Inclusivity

A common definition of inclusive is "to take in" or "to include". When something is exclusive, it usually indicates that it is excluded from some group, resulting in the sense of uniqueness due to the limited number of people allowed to participate. Being inclusive is often seen as the antithesis of being exclusive. Because anything is being included as a component of the whole, nothing can be left out of it. The concept of inclusivity is similar to that of forming a circle. All of the items that were mentioned before may be found inside it. People should believe that the world is one big circle in which practically everything exists, and they should make an effort to make that circle as inclusive as possible. "Open to everyone; not confined to select persons" is another way of saying "inclusive", which implies "encompassing everything". The term "exclusive" refers to anything that is "not shared" or "accessible to just a select few". When it comes to particular objects, persons, or groups, anything that is exclusive will exclude them.

Exclusivity in the term Patriarchy

The term patriarchy excluded the feminine gender. Many people think that patriarchy was a governmental framework that unequally distributed authority amongst males and females that was ultimately to the detriment of women. To put it another way, it refers to the uneven power structure that exists in many sectors of our cultures between men and women. Veronica Beechey, in her essay "On Patriarchy", states

Theoretically, the concept of patriarchy has been used to address the question of the real basis of the subordination of women and to analyse the particular forms which it assumes thus the theory of patriarchy attempts to penetrate beneath the particular experiences and manifestations of women's oppression and to formulate some coherent theory. (66)

Feminism sees patriarchy as an unfair social structure that still exists in the modern world that exclusively favours masculine gender and is not inclusive of the feminine gender. Carole Pateman writes, "The patriarchal construction of the difference between masculinity and femininity is the political difference between freedom and subjection (207)". Idea of patriarchy encompasses all of the public-political processes that are capable of being referred to as patriarchal institutions. These structures replicate and exert solely male inclusiveness while excluding women from participation. Patriarchy is often characterised as a social construction in feminist theory. It is argued that it may be abolished by exposing and critically evaluating patriarchy's many expressions and institutions. According to patriarchy, sexual and other ties between the sexes, regardless of whether or not they are acknowledged as such, are political relations through which men govern women. This is represented in the foundation of chauvinist communication, which defines masculine being the standard and that which includes or symbolises the feminine, and the feminine as "the other". In every instance of patriarchy that has been documented, negative connotations have been attached to women and the activities they engage in using symbols and myths. The descriptor "patriarchy" describes the systems or establishments that prevent females from taking part or staying in touch with spots of a greater authority or which are assumed as being the areas with the most power in terms of economics, politics, culture, and religion. "One alternative to patriarchy is to live within it in resistance" (Ruby 39). As the patriarchy excluded women, women started feminism in which they excluded and fought against men's dominance.

Exclusivity in the term Feminism

Feminism excluded the masculine gender, was inclusive only of women and was a reaction to the exclusion of women from patriarchy. For the last several decades, the field of feminist studies has been more interested in the investigation of feminist identity formation and the ways in which it impacts the lives of women. The process through which women come to accept and act upon feminist principles as a way of life is one definition of what is meant by the term 'feminist identity formation'. "Feminist theory should give voice to the previously silenced as well as increase understanding of their oppression" (Acker 235). Women are subjected to varying degrees of violence and diverse kinds of abuse throughout the spectrum of the patriarchy's many cultural, religious, and economic models. Some forms of abuse are universal, while others are exclusive to particular models of the patriarchy. The goal of feminism is to provide an all-encompassing explanation of the exclusion of women, including an explanation of its purported nature and genesis. The philosophy or theoretical commitment to women's inclusion and exclusion of men is known as feminism. "Revolutionary feminism has recently developed the radical feminist analysis of female subordination and claims that gender differences can be explained in terms of the biological differences between men and women. Revolutionary feminism develops a theory of patriarchy and sex class which is rooted in women's reproductive capacities" (Beechey 69). Mary Wollstonecraft, Simone de Beauvoir, Judith Butler, Donna J. Haraway, and Julia Kristeva are a few well-known feminists who have campaigned against the patriarchy's practice of excluding women from positions of power. Feminism excludes the masculine gender, includes only women, and fails to include homosexuals. So, gay/lesbian studies came up.

Exclusivity in the term Gay/Lesbian Studies

Gay/lesbian studies came up as an exclusion of all sexual orientations other than homosexuality. By the very term, everyone understands that it is an inclusive term just for gays and lesbians and excludes all other sexual orientations, including masculine and feminine. Lesbian is a term that is most often used as an exclusive term to describe a woman who has a romantic and/or sexual orientation toward other women. The term "gay" is used in various cultural contexts exclusively to refer to men who are romantically, erotically, or emotionally attracted to other males of the same gender. As a result of the fact that not all males who engage in sexual activity with others of the same gender consider themselves to be homosexual, it is important to use care when using this term. Some persons who do not identify as binary identifies with this phrase. These studies appeared in late 1970s in any form that could be considered structured. "Lesbian/gay studies owes its emergence to a series of intellectual developments that prepared the ground for its current expansion" (Weston 341). Gay men, lesbians, and their allies began openly and self-consciously studying themselves and how they were represented in history and culture with the advent of the gay liberation movement. This led them to inquire how gender and sexual orientations have been constructed and conceptualised in the past and how they are being constructed and conceptualised in the present. The essays "One is Not Born a Woman" by Monique Wittig (1981), Teresa de Lauretis' "Sexual Indifference and Lesbian Representation" (1988) and "Commodity Lesbianism" by Danae Clark (1991) all make significant contributions to the field of lesbian studies. Wittig's essay "One is Not Born a Woman" offers an alternative to previous explanations of the historical causes of gender exclusion. Gay/lesbian studies included only gay and lesbian and excluded bisexuals and transgenders. Therefore LGBT, which is inclusive of Bisexuals and transgenders, came up.

Exclusivity in the Acronym LGBT

The Term LGBT included only Lesbians, Gays, Bisexuals and Transgender and excluded all others. The researcher has already mentioned about gays and lesbians, and therefore only the meanings of the terms bisexuality and transgender are explored here. A person is said to be bisexual if they have a sexual, romantic, physical, and spiritual attraction to people of both sexes. However, these types of attraction do not need to occur simultaneously, in the same manner, or to the same degree. The term bisexual is used exclusively for the persons who engage in sex or are attracted to both feminine and masculine gender, but it excludes all other sexual orientations. A person is considered to be transgender if their sense of personal identification or gender does not match to the sex they were given at birth or if they do not comply with traditional gender norms. Sexual orientation varies and is not reliant on gender identity. Transgender is also an exclusive term that focuses only on transgender persons and excludes all other orientations. As the terms patriarchy, feminism, gay/lesbian studies, and LGBT were exclusive terms; the word queer came up as an inclusive term that encompasses all sexual orientations.

Exclusive Inclusivity in the Term Queer

"Queer methodologies have opened up myriad avenues of productive scholarly in- quiry into literature and culture, thanks to the fluidity of the very word queer" (Stewart 204). The term queer is an inclusive term comprising all sexual inclinations. As Hanson states, "queer theory marks out a "domain virtually synonymous with homosexuality and yet wonderfully suggestive of a whole range of sexual possibilities that challenge the familiar distinction between normal and pathological, straight and gay, masculine men and feminine women" (138). The term queer is called as an inclusive term because it includes all the sexual orientations and excludes none. Jackson and Jones state that "anyone who feels at odds with the social or sexual convention can claim the label "queer", including, presumably, heterosexual men" (124). The phrase "queer theory" refers to a body of work that investigates the lives all people. This collection of work has been referred to as "queer theory". In a broader sense, queer theory has investigated the processes at play within modern society when it comes to constructing sexual identities. Within this context, queer theory has pushed anti-essentialist assertions about the cultural formation of sexual identities, particularly the variety and ambivalence of these identities. The study of the queer theory involves doing an analytical investigation into the mechanisms through which power is used to institutionalise and legitimise some kinds and manifestations of sexuality at the same time stigmatising the rest.

The development of Queer Theory in academic circles coincided with the growing prominence of Gay and Lesbian Studies. "Queer is intended to remedy what some believe to be the intellectual and political limitations of the identity-based categories "gay" and "lesbian"" (Penn and Irvine 329). Queer theory problematises and criticises inflexible norms and oppressions. In contrast, LGBT Studies aims to understand LGBT persons as unwavering distinctiveness; queer Theory questions and confronts these ideas. Queer theory, sometimes called the "deconstruction" of LGBT studies, destabilises identities by permitting and promoting diverse explanations of social events that are not constrained in any way. It is based on the premise that all sexual behaviours and expressions of gender are built in a social context and breed methods of societal connotation. Sarah Schulman, the American queer writer, uses non-heterosexual themes in her novels especially in *Girls, Visions and Everything, After Delores, People In Trouble, Empathy, Rat Bohemia,* and *The Child*. As her themes in these in novels include homosexuality, heterosexuality, and pornography and so on, she can rightly be called as an advocate of queer individual's rights and privileges.

Conclusion

This research analysed the terms patriarchy, feminism, gay/ lesbian studies, LGBT as exclusive terms and Queer as an inclusive term. It has defined the meaning of inclusivity and exclusivity. Patriarchy is an exclusive term that refers to the masculine gender. Feminism is another exclusive term that includes the feminine gender. Gay/Lesbian studies is an exclusive term that includes only homosexuals. LGBT is another exclusive term that comprises only Lesbians, gays, Bisexuals and Transgender. Queer is the only term that is inclusive of all sexual orientations. The term queer is seen as an exclusive inclusive term that includes all sexual orientations. People envision a world of inclusivity that promotes inclusion, equilibrium, equality and peace and not exclusivity that promotes injustice and inequality.

References

- Acker, Joan. " The Problem with Patriarchy." *Sociology*, vol. 23, no. 2, 1989, pp. 235–40. *JSTOR*, www.jstor.org/stable/42853922.
- Beechey, Veronica. "On Patriarchy." *Feminist Review*, no. 3, 1979, pp. 66–82. *JSTOR*, doi.org/10.2307/1394710.
- Jackson, Stevi, and Jackie Jones, eds. *Contemporary feminist theories*. Edinburgh University Press, 1998.
- Pateman, Carole. *The Sexual Contract*, Stanford University Press, 1988.
- Penn, Donna, and Janice Irvine. "Gay/Lesbian/Queer Studies." *Contemporary Sociology*, vol. 24, no. 3, 1995, pp. 328–30. *JSTOR*, doi.org/10.2307/2076480.
- Ruby, Jennie. "Resistances To Patriarchy." *Off Our Backs*, vol. 33, no. 3/4, 2003, pp. 38–40. JSTOR, www.jstor.org/stable/20837789.
- Stewart, Faye. "Queer Approaches." *The German Quarterly*, vol. 91, no. 2, 2018, pp. 204–07. JSTOR, www.jstor.org/stable/44974033.
- Weston, Kath. "Lesbian/Gay Studies in the House of Anthropology." *Annual Review of Anthropology*, vol. 22, 1993, pp. 339–67. JSTOR, www.jstor.org/stable/2155852.

---

[1]**Joseph K. J.,** is aResearch Scholar, Department of English, St. Joseph's College (Autonomous) Trichy - 620002, Best Research Scholar 2023, AIFEST International Poetry Competition 'A' Grade Winner, ICSSR Fellowship 2022-23.

[2]**Dr. J. Amalaveenus,** Assistant Professor and Research Guide, Department of English, St. Joseph's College (Autonomous) Trichy - 620002

• • •

Rising of Popular Literary Devices (Stream of Consciousness) in "The Dark Holds No Terror" by Shashi Deshpande

J. Revathy[1] and Dr. Murugavel S.[2]

[1]Research Scholar, The Department of English, Vel Tech Rangarajan Dr.Sagunthala R&D Institute of Science and Technology, Avadi, Chennai- 62

[2]Research Supervisor, Assistant Professor, The Department of English, Vel Tech Rangarajan Dr.Sagunthala R&D Institute of Science and Technology, Avadi, Chennai - 62

Abstract

The Stream of Consciousness is one of the frequently employed literary techniques by Indian writers of English. Shashi Deshpande mostly addressed feminist concerns with the 'Stream of Consciousness' narrative technique. The term "Stream of Consciousness" initially appears in the late 19th century to assist the research of an original, self-aware subjectivity. Psychological expression was used to describe a specific novelistic or characterization strategy that was prevalent in many fictional works. Shashi Deshpande explores the present-day thought processes of her characters by utilizing the literary device known as The Stream of consciousness. She uses this technique in the novel "The Dark Holds No Terror," and makes her readers get into her protagonist's mind. Her female protagonists are victims of the prevailing gender discrimination, first as daughters and later as wives. The protagonist "Saru" serves as the narrator. She is a middle-class Indian woman. She rebels against societal norms and customs while attempting to reach a compromise with the circumstances of the time. This is largely because she is living through a period of transition. She thoroughly enters the minds of the women and introduces a new morality. She was successful in transforming the protagonist "Saur's" wordless anguish into repulsive thinking to develop her individuality.

Keywords: The Stream of consciousness, Feministic, Narrative Technique, Transitional, Identity.

Introduction

The Stream of Consciousness Narrative Technique appears in the late nineteenth century in favor of the exploration of personal and self-conscious subjectivity. It is a style of writing used by many great authors during the modern period.It reflects the flow of the character's thoughts and feelings. By using the Stream of Consciousness Narrative Technique Shashi Deshpande traces the mental process of her characters that are contemporary. According to Shashi Deshpande, a modern woman's existence is complicated. She strives to be "All in One," a modern woman who is also traditional. However, in reality, nothing is ever that easy. To make room for anything new, one must let go of the old. Through the protagonist 'Saru' in The Dark Holds No Terrors, Shashi Deshpande has been able to reveal the inner sentiments of Indian women from all walks of life. She is successful in the novel in turning Saru's wordless pain into disgusting thoughts and her right to achieve her own identity.

The Stream of Consciousness

The phrase was first used by Alexander Bain in his 1855 novel "The Senses and the Intellect."The philosopher and psychologist William James' book "The Principles of Psychology" published in the 1890s contain the first instance of it.

Consciousness, then, does not appear to itself as chopped up in bits . . . it is nothing

joined; it flows a 'river' or a 'stream' are the metaphors by which it is most naturally

described. In talking about it hereafter, let's call it the stream of thought, consciousness,

or subjective life. . . (James 39).

The Stream of Consciousness is a literary method that depicts a character's view. In literature, the term "Stream of Consciousness" first appears in the late nineteenth century to encourage the examination of a unique, conscious subjectivity. Some novelists frequently associate this literary writing style with the modernist movement. The authors of the School of Stream of Consciousness wrote in a compressed or blocked style. It is irrational and inadequately defined which causes a tremendous lot of complications for the reader. The psychological phrase was used to characterize a specific novelistic or characterization method that appeared frequently in literary works. In "The Dark Holds No Terrors" Shashi Deshpande employs The Stream of Consciousness narrative approach which deals with the flow of ideas, thoughts, feelings, and sensations in the fictional style of writing. Shashi Deshpande made an effort to develop deeper into the characters' minds.

Shashi Deshpande

Shashi Deshpande is one of the famous writers in Indian writing in English. Her journey started as a Journalist for the magazine "Onlooker" in Mumbai while attending the Vidya Bhavan to study journalism. Then she was interested in writing Short stories, which were first released as a collection in 1978. Her first Novel "The Dark Holds No Terror" was published in 1980. She received the Sahitya Akademi Award in 1990 and Padma Shri Award in 2009 for the novel "That Long Silence". She was shortlisted for The Hindu Literary Prize in 2014 for her work, "Shadow Play". Shashi Deshpande has written four children's books, several short stories, thirteen novels, and an essay collection entitled 'Writing from the Margin and Other Essays'. In her novels, she explores the inner lives of Indian women. She gives genuine portrayals of her heroines. Feminism as practiced by Shashi Deshpande is by no means cynical. She goes beyond the feminist approach by analyzing the problem of the woman in terms of its global relevance.

The Dark Holds No Terror:

It was published in 1980. It has been translated into German and Russian. This is Shashi Deshpande's First and dearest novel as she said in an interview:

"It has a simple theme and fewer characters. It gripped me so much that

I whipped through the writing, the wife had a better job and there was a very obvious

tension between them. He was aggressive and surly. That set it off." (Times of India, 22)

'The Dark Holds No Terror' narrates the story of a marriage on the rocks. The protagonist Saritha is a successful lady doctor. It tells of the conflict that she has to face as a doctor and as a wife. From Childhood she was accused by her mother of her brother's death. Even after her marriage, Saru herself doesn't feel content with her life and family. She feels as if she has been lost in an alien land. Shashi Deshpande uses 'The Stream of Consciousness' to make Saru recall her childhood experiences, and estranged relationship with her mother, her marriage with the handsome young poet, Manohar and the suffering which follows, and her relationship with her daughter Renu and son Abhi. The novel opens with Saru's return to her maternal home.

'It was The Krishna Sudama story that suddenly came to her mind that illustration

Which had accompanied the story about Queen Rukmini running joyously to

Greet poor, ragged Sudama standing at the palace gates. As she knocked at the door,

She wondered why the story had come back to her mind. She was certainly no

Sudama in rags, bare feet and humility. She had none of these. She has one suitcase

of clothes.'(Deshpande1980:15)

Saru was thinking about her childhood days when she sat for lunch in the kitchen. Her mother had erased Saru from her household except for a photograph only because Dhruva was in it too. Saru was depicted by Shashi Deshpande using psychological principles; although being well educated, Saru has fallen victim to sentimental ideals as a result of her memories of her mother and her childhood in her home. Her mother says,

"You killed him. Why didn't you die? Why are you alive, when he is dead?" (P191).

At one occurrence, Saru unconsciously thinks of her dead brother Dhurva, she is interrupted by her father and Madhav. She thinks that Dhurva is not Madhav sitting on Baba's lap and talking to him.

'And I had thought...and I must show Baba something, to take his attention away

from Dhruva sitting on his lap. I must make him listen to me, not to Dhruva. I must

make ignores Dhruva. But she had not succeeded. The memory became

hazy again.' (P 32)

Saru remembers the bitter words of her mother that followed her for days, months, and years, through her life. The incident made Saru's life more desperate. Her mother consistently longs for her deceased son and disapproves of even her daughter's presence. The young Saru is filled with sentiments of hatred for her mother. Saru is continuously thinking about her mother's advice. Death seals off all possibilities of straightening things. Dead or alive, Saru sees the mother slapping her of all happiness and asks herself.

'There were only the two of us. when Dhruva died, there was only me. But if there

Were any burdens on me, I threw them off, and she died alone. Didn't she mind that?

Was it, not her failure too' (P31)

Shashi Deshpande has presented a devastating effect on Saru through the partisan attitude of her mother. She was haunted by the thought that she is responsible for her brother's death. Saru's love dreams begin and end with Manohar. He was uncomfortable with Saru's steady rise in status, as a famous Doctor, he felt ignored when people greeted and paid attention to Saru. She feels a gradual disappearance of love and attachment toward her husband and children. She wants her father to support her. She blurts loudly and crudely, "My husband is a sadist."(P199) In her father's house, she has time to review her relationship not only with her husband, her dead mother, her brother Dhruva, her grandmother, and her children Renu and Abhi. The day they were to take Abhi for his vaccination when she saw them preparing him and themselves, she had suddenly skipped to her mother, a child again, not a grave, withdrawn person, and said,

"Oh, are we going to return him now looking as if happen was again within her

Reaching it had scared her. Dhruva and I ... Dhruva and I ....did I push him?

The question sprang her out of nothing, again and again... did I? Did I?"(P72)

At the end of the novel, Saru tried to make a compromise with the situation. There was a hope of resettlement. She revolts against the traditional life of married women and their practice, but ultimately tries to compromise with reality. All women are raising their voices only for the voiceless. Through the Stream of Consciousness narrative technique, her works have helped all of us to break the silence and the chains on several social issues.

Conclusion

Shashi Deshpande's novels fully depict the psychoanalytic study of human relations and human issues. She has managed to bring forth the inner thoughts of Indian women from all walks of life.

Her female characters rebel against social restrictions and old conventions. They struggle for their freedom, completeness and identity and subsist in opposition to the existing system and tradition of society to express their feelings, anger and indignation against the social taboos, but it does not bring any satisfaction. Any woman who reads her book will in some way recognize herself in it. Sigmund Freud and Ernst Mach's theories have an impact on contemporary literature. According to their views, the mind is constantly active, and everything that goes through it aids in our ability to perceive the outside world. Utilizing women's strengths helps them to achieve their personal goals and benefits society. When they identified, they experienced happiness in their own lives. Through this sense of self, women resemble free-spirited males. They have made a name for themselves as independent people. Women can be conscious of their own needs and rights. By raising awareness among the oppressed women, these ladies established themselves as role models.

References

- Deshpande, Shashi. "The Dark holds no terror" India: Penguin Books, 1980.Print
- Naik, M.K. "Dimensions of Indian English Literature". New Delhi: Sterling Publishers, 1985. Print.
- Interview by M. D. Rati. "I'm not a feminist: Shashi Deshpande." Times of India. 22 July 2001. Web, 7 Jan. 2016.
- James, William. "The Principles of Psychology" 1890 New York: Dover Publication, 1950 Print.

• • •

CHAPTER XV

Manumission in the form of The Day in Shadow by Nayantara Sahgal

K. Siva Madasamy[1] and Dr. V. Chanthiramathi[2]

[1]PhD Research Scholar (Full-Time), Reg.No: 21112234011014, P.G and Research Department of English, V.O. Chidambaram College, Thoothukudi – 628008, Affiliated to Manonmaniam Sundaranar University, Tirunelveli

[2]Research Guide, P.G and Research Department of English, V.O. Chidambaram College, Thoothukudi – 628008, Affiliated to Manonmaniam Sundaranar University, Tirunelveli.

In this paper, the finding emphases the Manumission and the identity crises of a liberated woman in Nayantara Sahgal's novel The Day in Shadow. Her writing is a combination of feminism and politics. This novel focuses on the life of Simrit, a young and divorced woman who lives in a judgmental society in India. It is a stereotypical society that continues to subjugate women in all ways, preaching that women are always subservient to their males. The author communicates her personal unpleasant marriage experience through the female character Simrit. As the protagonist of the novel, Simrit deals with, struggles with, and supports herself after a failed marriage. Because of the divorce, she becomes an independent woman who breaks free from the oppressed and subjugated as a married woman in a society dominated by men. This research covers the challenges of divorced women in patriarchal culture, as well as the violent marriage settlement following divorce, confirming the title's claim that Simrit experiences a Manumission and identity crisis throughout the work. However, this study is far more significant because of its theme, which symbolizes one of the most prevalent challenges experienced by women in marriage in finding an identity for oneself in order to live a happy life. Through her writing of fictional characters and historical events, Sahgal discusses all themes of politics, social concerns, religion, ethics, cultural diversity, feminism, and Gandhian philosophy.

Simrit, the story's protagonist, is unloved, traumatised, and constrained by her memories of domestic violence. Her selfish husband, Som, with whom she shares an incompatible relationship, also treats her unfairly and represses her memories. To establish a new life, she crosses paths with Raj, a clever person aspiring to become a member of parliament. This finding focuses around how the character Simrit finds happiness and self-identity despite her challenges both domestically and politically as a divorcee in an Indian society dominated by males. Since Sahgal is a socio-political author, the study makes an effort to compare the husband-wife relationship tales in the novel. The work makes an effort to debate and examine the writer's autobiographical narratives.

The issue of identity crisis and women's battles to break out from disastrous marriages and live a financially and psychologically independent existence is depicted through this novel. Sahgal employed an allegorical stream of consciousness style and approach to represent the protagonist of the novel Simrit. Sahgal's novels depict the contemporary political scenarios, including the dark side of corruption, dominance, and using the power against women, ministers or parliament members abusing their positions, and the subjugation of women in patriarchal societies that portray women as toys, materials, or property. Her works paint a vivid picture of women's condition in Post-Independence India. She depicts how women in patriarchal culture lose their identity and self-esteem, to becoming silent and puppets to their men.

The evil side of corruption, dominance and the abuse of authority against the weak, ministerial or parliamentary abuse of position, and the exploitation of women in patriarchal societies that see them as objects, commodities, or property are all shown in Sahgal's works. Her books paint a rich portrait of women's situation in post-independence India. She illustrates how, in a patriarchal culture, women lose their sense of themselves and self-respect, and turn into puppets of their men.

Simrit is a typical representation of an Indian married woman imprisoned to her four walls. She picked a non-Brahmin person as her soul mate despite coming from a traditional Brahmin family background, but subsequently realized that their bonding style was radically different. She feels incompatible and angry over her choice to marry a non-Brahmin. The study focuses on analyzing Simrit's post-divorce challenges and issues in patriarchal society. How she undergoes a transformative stage in order to become a new woman. The bulk of the female characters in Sahgal's novel come from rich backgrounds. Despite their education and upbringing, they are still treated as inferior to men and are expected to accept their fate without question. They also frequently have the wrong kind of marriage arrangements. However, some of her protagonists, such as Simrit in The Day in Shadow, and Rashmi in This Time in Morning decide to have a divorce in order to achieve independence and overcome taboos associated with Indian marriage.

The female lead in Sahgal's stories plays a significant role in the development of the new woman idea in India. Her female characters are married, either divorced, or single women to strive better themselves as liberated people while battling for equality and a voice of the society that is mostly masculine. We can see that Sahgal applies Gandhi's philosophy to feminism because she wants women to have free, happy lives with their husbands through good understanding and communication in all spheres of their lives psychologically, financially, emotionally, and socially.

" I try to create the virtuous woman the modern Site, if you like. My women are strivers and aspirers, toward freedom, toward goodness, toward a compassionate world. Their virtue is a quality of heart and mind and spirit, a kind of untouched innocence and integrity. I think there is this quality in the Indian woman" (45).

The main characters of the novel are Simrit and Som, whose marriage was initially happy and comfortable. However, Simrit later discovers that she and Som have a mismatched marriage bond because Som doesn't fully understand her and treats her more like a sexual object than as a partner in a loving relationship. Since he forces and oppresses her to make decisions about domestic duties and other matters, she feels mistrust and disappointment towards him. Simrit is the sort of woman who wants to be in a relationship that provides her independence, equality, and respect. This connection should be kind of understanding, love, kindness, and excellent bonding. However, Som treats her poorly, treating her like a sexual object. He is the sort of ambitious, materialistic person who wants Simrit to be like him in return. The lines make this very clear. "Som's world had been commerce, never shared with her at all". (12).

Simrit is anxious and isolated from Som as a result of these psychological pressures. She alienates herself from him by not pleasing him sexually; remaining separated which leads to divorce. Simrit desired a life of independence, identity, and uniqueness, as well as excellent communication between them, but Som's materialistic mentality set the ground for separation in their lives. When Som forces her to buy chair coverings and curtains for the house, she feels physically and emotionally constrained, distrusted, and pushed. She felt as if she was losing her sense of self and identity as this connection became more entrenched in her life. Som keeps the servant after Simrit dismisses him for drinking. The suffocation and insult faced by her are conveyed through the following passage:

"She hadn't. Not even about chair covers and curtains. Even there Som had had a veto. Not even about servants. She had dismissed the cook twice for drunkenness and bad behavior and Som had kept him on. Little things, she had thought at the time, nothing important, nothing to quarrel about, but building up into a frightening situation—herself a cog in a machine—with which it had become impossible to live". (38).

Simrit is the person who wants everything to be in order and well planned, but Som constantly silences her. When Raj asks her of her purpose for life after her divorce, she responded permanence. She stated that this is what she wished for.

"I've wanted everything to be same forever, furniture never moved from its place, never changing address, children growing older in the same house, a godown where tons of could collect and not be in anybody's way, and not lose prestige, you know just because ther're a bit battered and old and where one could find them years later: toys and souvenirs and old report cards and that sort of things. Life should be—continuous". (37).

Through the novel's character Raj, Sahgal criticizes the lack of uniqueness and identity in women's lives. "Had she ever been avid, really avid about anything at all? She simply could not go through life like this, letting other people's ambitions and actions overwhelm her. First it had been her husband. Next, it could be her children. Woman for use had been the rule too long". (38).

Raj is the only person who cares about Simrit's originality, independence, and educated intellect; Raj is also the only one who has fired her writing aspiration. Sahgal is a firm believer in her idea that it is not immoral to defy convention by loving someone else again after a divorce, rather than accepting and living a destiny of mismatched married life. Simrit is an educated, tolerant, open-minded, and a feminist, yet it took her a long time to select divorce as a path to freedom. Later, Raj's brave and courageous statements inspired her to choose divorce in order to effectively leave an oppressive unsuitable marriage bond.

"In this society with no social security, Sahgal portrays the social miseries of being a divorcee. Economically, the painful marital settlement that imposes taxes on it" which generates an extra financial problem for her is the worst psychological burden she endured during her divorce. Through the character Simrit, she addresses these socio-economic challenges auto-biographically. Simrit's life was full of superior comfort until her divorce. However, because of the harsh divorce settlement, Simrit is left to fend for herself in terms of food, bills, children, and tax issues. "All the living wealth and has left behind the crockery and furniture and liven and jewels and sliver som got all thing, the cars, the bank accounts" (58). Som expects Simrit to surrender to him: "Som could have forgiven her if she had been a weaker being, unsure, dependent and even deceiving, but beneath her docility she was none of these things unpardonable" (53).

However, Simrit had financial success despite her struggles. Simirit recognizes that she wants a partner who can provide her with emotional and psychological trust, independence, equality, and a sense of originality. Fortunately, she found Raj, who can provide just that. Simrit, her kids, and the tax are all accepted by Raj with all of his affection. Giving her own uniqueness and personality, he expresses her love without holding anything back.

Nayantara Sahgal believes that women and men should live equal and harmonious lives. The novel The Day in Shadow paints a realistic image of New Woman through the heroine Simrit, a powerful woman who chooses divorce over a male-centered, subordinated life. In this novel, Simrit properly expresses Sahgal's point of view on feminism in marriage. Simrit evolved as a New Woman with autonomous and feminine ideas, both economically and mentally, following her transition phase. Simrit's self-realization, identity, and bravery pave the way for women to prioritize womanhood in all parts of their lives in order to live a happy and fulfilled life.

References

- Sahgal, Nayantara. The Day in Shadow. Penguin random house pvt. Ltd. Print. 1991
- Jain, Jabir, Nayantara Sahgal New Delhi: Arnold Heinemann, 1978, p.45
- https://www.the-criterion.com/nayantara-sahgals-rich-like-us-a-thematic-analysis/
- http://www.rjelal.com/6.1.18/220-223%20PRASATH.K.pdf
- https://www.researchgate.net/publication/344498890_Exploring_Identity_Crisis_in_Nayantara_Sahgal%27s_Day_in_Shadow
- https://journalppw.com/index.php/jpsp/article/view/5438/3597

K. Siva Madasamy, is a Ph.D. Full- Time Research Scholar working under the guidance of Dr V. Chanthiramathi at V. O. Chidambaram College, Tuticorin, Tamil Nadu, India. He is doing his research on Indian Writing in English. His area of interest is Indian Writing in English, American Literature, and Dalit Literature.

Dr. V. Chanthiramathi, is an Associate Professor of English at V. O. Chidambaram College, Tuticorin, Tamil Nadu, India. She has been teaching English Language and Literature for 22 years. She is a research adviser and has guided Thirty M.Phil. Scholars and Twenty-Two Ph. D. Scholars. She is guiding four Ph. D. Scholars at present. She has organized many National level seminars and workshops funded by UGC and Tamil Nadu State Council for Higher Education, Chennai. Her area of specialization is American Literature and Indian Writing in English.

• • •

CHAPTER XVI

Homonationalism: A Theoretical Understanding of Gender and Homonormativity as National Identities in the Select Bollywood Movies

Padmapriya P.[1] and Dr. A. Ganesan[2]

[1]*Research Scholar, Department of EFL, SRM IST. Tamilnadu, India*

[2]*Associate Professor, Department of English, RKM Vivekananda College. Tamilnadu, India*

Abstract

The concept of 'nation' and 'nationalism' plays an indispensable role in the formation of the national identity of its citizens. Movies function as a key position in mass media communication. The plot, thoughts, characters and other features of a film serve as a medium through which information is conveyed to the audience and occasionally generate social transformation. As a result, the portrayal of gender in movies is one of the strongest methods of teaching "What is gender?". By emphasising heterosexuality as heteronormativity, movies not only reinforce patriarchy but also foster antipathy toward homosexuals. This can be accomplished by including xenophobic and homophobic themes, images, and circumstances in the plot. The researchers aim to understand how Lesbian, Gay, Transgender, and other genders are delineated in films as comedic figures, villains, and other humiliating characters, reflecting the heteronormative society's concept of 'others'. The examination of xenophobic and homophobic notions and picturisation in Bollywood films trace the historical evolution of Nation and National identities through the lens of Jasbir K Puar's homonationalism. Furthermore, this research paper seeks to observe homonationalist beliefs in Bollywood films as a contributing element to the spread of homonationalism.

Keywords: Homonationalism, Bollywood Movies, Xenophobia, Homophobia, Normativity

---

Media play a major role in influencing the mind of people. Mass media not only entertain but also educate the minds consciously and unconsciously. Within mass media, movies hold an indispensable role in entertaining the audience and influencing humans to align themselves with what is normal and what is abnormal in society. This normativity is found in the actions of humans in building their identities of what is a man and what is a woman. As media is the source of information we are dependent upon, it is a support to the people for shaping their opinions and attitudes (Keswani et al.). Bollywood movies significantly impact the portrayal and perception of gender roles in Indian society. Through their stories, characters, and depictions, for instance, in many Bollywood movies, men are often portrayed as strong, dominant figures who are the providers and protectors of their families, while women are depicted as emotional, submissive, and often dependent on men. This portrayal reinforces the idea that men are naturally suited to take on leadership roles while women are meant to be supportive and nurturing., Bollywood movies often reinforce traditional gender stereotypes and expectations.

In alignment with the projection of women, the projection of transgender in the media creates a stereotype that justifies and picturises them as non-normative in the heteronormative society. Bollywood movies have often portrayed transgender people in a negative light. Thus, this has been done mainly to drive the plot of the movie, often involving comedic relief or shock value. This portrayal is inaccurate and insensitive, perpetuating dangerous stereotypes and ignorance about the transgender community. This negative portrayal reinforces harmful stereotypes and reinforces the marginalisation of the transgender community in Indian society. In many cases, transgender characters are depicted as objects of ridicule, violence, or sexual exploitation. In the movie "Dolly Ki Doli" (2015), in which a transgender person is portrayed as a criminal who tricks unsuspecting grooms into marrying her. The character is portrayed as deceitful and morally bankrupt, perpetuating harmful stereotypes about transgender individuals. Another movie, "Waqt: The Race Against Time" (2005), is in which a transgender character is portrayed as a clown-like figure who is subjected to ridicule and violence. In the movie "Kalank" (2019), there is a mention of a transgender character who is portrayed as a "devious" figure. In the film "Kabir Singh" (2019), there is also a negative portrayal of a transgender character. In the film "Sajjan Singh Rangroot" (2018), a transgender character is depicted as a beggar in the streets. In the film "Padmaavat" (2018), the character of Begum Qilich Khan is shown to be a transgender character who is a negative influence. These negative portrayals of transgender individuals in Bollywood movies contribute to a culture of discrimination and stigma towards the transgender community.

The portrayal of lesbian relationships in Bollywood movies has been limited and stereotypical. In the past, same-sex relationships were not depicted openly and were often portrayed in a negative light. For example, in the movie "Fire" (1996), two women who are unhappily married to men enter into a romantic relationship with each other. However, the film portrays their relationship as driven by lust and lack of fulfillment in their marriages, rather than genuine affection and love for each other. The film also portrays their relationship as being morally wrong, and the consequences of their relationship are shown as negative, contributing to the perpetuation of harmful stereotypes about lesbian relationships.

The portrayal of gay relationships in Bollywood has been limited and stereotypical, much like that of lesbian relationships. They are portrayed in a negative light, with gay characters being portrayed as humorous caricatures or as villains. In the movie "Dostana" (2008), where one of the male characters pretends to be gay to rent an apartment with his straight best friend, the characters often use effeminate mannerisms and camp behaviour for comedic effect. In another movie, "Kal Ho Naa Ho" (2003), where a character is depicted as being gay but is portrayed as being diseased and sad, ultimately leading to his tragic death. These stereotypical and negative portrayals reinforce harmful societal attitudes towards the LGBTQ+ community and perpetuate discrimination against them.

Achieving transgender inclusion in our society requires a multi-faceted approach. It includes creating a society where gender identity is respected and accepted, advocating for legal recognition of transgender persons, providing access to healthcare and other services, and raising awareness of transgender issues. Additionally, open communication and dialogue between transgender persons and their allies can be beneficial in advancing progress on this issue. Further, transphobia can be removed from society through education and awareness. Educating people on the subject of gender identity, gender expression, and individual rights can help them understand why transphobia is wrong and why it should not be tolerated. Additionally, raising public awareness of the issue through campaigns, public discussions, and media coverage can help create a more inclusive and understanding environment for everyone.

Jasbir K. Puar's concept of homonationalism refers to the way that LGBTQ rights have been co-opted to serve a wider nationalist agenda. Specifically, they argue that in many Western countries, LGBTQ+ rights are used to promote a sense of exceptionalism and superiority in comparison to other nations. Thus, this includes countries with anti-LGBTQ+ laws or policies, which are highlighted to contrast and justify the rights of LGBTQ+ people in the West. This leads to a form of "homonationalism" that reinforces existing systems of power. Homonationalism is an idea in queer theory that suggests that some members of the LGBTQ+ people are represented in all aspects of society, from politics to business, to help combat stereotypes and prejudice.

Homonationalism is also used to describe the idea that LGBTQ+ people must identify with the nation-state in order to gain their rights and recognition. This concept of nationhood is based on the assumption that LGBTQ+ people should be seen as citizens who can contribute to the nation and be treated with respect. This idea has been widely studied and discussed in recent years and is used to examine the relationship between national identity and LGBT rights. Transgender people are slowly beginning to be more visible in mainstream Bollywood movies; however, they are still largely underrepresented, and their stories are often sensationalised and stereotypical. Transgender characters in Bollywood movies are often portrayed as comedic relief or in melodramatic roles as outcasts - often as victims of abuse or discrimination. They are often seen as victims of society or objects of pity or sympathy. Recent Bollywood movies have tried to break this stereotype by portraying transgender characters in more empowering roles, with stories of hope and resilience.

In recent years, a few movies have attempted to tell stories of transgender people in a more sensitive, authentic, and nuanced way. In the past, transgender characters were often portrayed as clowns or villains, but today they are portrayed as more rounded characters with their own motivations and desires. In some recent movies, transgender characters have even become protagonists, leading the story and accurately representing transgender people.

However, in recent years, there has been a shift towards more progressive and accepting portrayals of lesbian relationships in Bollywood movies, although they remain few and far between. Several films have presented positive portrayals of LGBTQ+ characters, which has helped normalise them in society. One of the more notable examples of a positive portrayal of a lesbian relationship in Bollywood is the movie "Ek Ladki Ko Dekha Toh

Aisa Laga" (2019), which tells the story of a young woman coming out to her conservative Punjabi family. The film received widespread critical acclaim for handling the subject matter and breaking taboos around same-sex relationships in India. The film portrays same-sex love in a sensitive and non-stereotypical way, while also addressing important issues such as family pressure and societal expectations. Another film with a positive portrayal of LGBTQ+ characters is "Kapoor & Sons" (2016), which features a gay character who is a writer and has a loving relationship with his partner. The film showcases their relationship as normal and loving, like any other relationship. The storyline deals with their struggles to come out to their families, but the film's overall message is acceptance and love.

"Shubh Mangal Zyada Saavdhan" (2020) is another recent Bollywood film that presents a positive image of gay relationships and tackles issues such as homophobia and societal acceptance. The film features an engaged gay couple who want to get married but face opposition from their families. These films, and several others like them, showcase LGBTQ+ characters as positive, loving, and deserving of respect and acceptance. They have helped to break stereotypes and prejudices while educating audiences about the complexities of LGBTQ+ experiences. Furthermore, in recent years, films such as these have helped create a more inclusive society where people of all backgrounds and orientations can feel validated and accepted. Despite these positive developments, there is still a long way to go in terms of creating authentic, nuanced and positive portrayals of lesbian relationships in Bollywood movies. Nevertheless, it is important to note that representation matters and the increasing visibility of same-sex relationships in Indian cinema can have a significant impact on changing public attitudes towards the LGBTQ+ community.

In conclusion, movies play a significant role in shaping societal attitudes towards gender and sexuality. The negative portrayal of transgender individuals and LGBTQ+ relationships in Bollywood movies perpetuates harmful stereotypes and reinforces discrimination against them. This research paper has traced the historical evolution of the nation and national identities through the lens of homonationalism and observed homonationalist beliefs in Bollywood films as a contributing factor to the spread of homonationalism. Achieving transgender inclusion in our society requires a multi-faceted approach, including creating a society where gender identity is respected and accepted, advocating for legal recognition of transgender rights, and increasing positive representation of transgender individuals in the media. It is essential to create a culture of acceptance and tolerance towards all individuals, regardless of their gender identity or sexual orientation. Finally, filmmakers have a significant responsibility in promoting social justice and equality in their work, and their positive contributions can help to create a more inclusive society.

References

- *Dolly Ki Doli.* Abhishek Dogra, Sonam Kapoor, Pulkit Samrat, Rajkummar Rao, and Varun Sharma, *Arbaaz Khan Productions*, 2015.
- *Dostana.* Directed by Tarun Mansukhani, performances by Abhishek Bachchan, John Abraham, and Priyanka Chopra, *Dharma Productions*, 2008.
- *Ek Ladki Ko Dekha Toh Aisa Laga.* Directed by Shelly Chopra Dhar, performances by Sonam Kapoor, Anil Kapoor, Rajkummar Rao, Juhi Chawla, and Regina Cassandra, *Vidhu Vinod Chopra Productions*, 2019.
- *Kabir Singh.* Sandeep Reddy Vanga, Shahid Kapoor and Kiara Advani, *T-Series*, 2019.
- *Kalank.* Abhishek Varman, Madhuri Dixit, Sonakshi Sinha, Alia Bhatt, Varun Dhawan, Aditya Roy Kapur, and Sanjay Dutt, *Dharma Productions*, 2019.
- *Kal Ho Naa Ho.* Directed by Nikkhil Advani, performances by Shah Rukh Khan, Preity Zinta, and Saif Ali Khan, *Dharma Productions*, 2003.

- Kapoor, K. (2017). "Representation of Gender Roles in Bollywood Films: A Study of Bollywood as a Reflection of Society". *The Journal of Arts and Humanities*, 6(3), 37-47.
- *Kapoor & Sons*. Directed by Shakun Batra, performances by Rishi Kapoor, Sidharth Malhotra, Fawad Khan, and Alia Bhatt, *Dharma Productions*, 2016.
- Keswani, Saumya & Kattu, Kushagra & Wani, Abrar & Balamurugan, J. (2018). Effect of Mass Media on Objectifying of Humans. 14-18.
- Lauren B. McInroy & Shelley L. Craig (2015) Transgender Representation in Offline and Online Media: LGBTQ Youth Perspectives, *Journal of Human Behavior in the Social Environment*, 25:6, 606-617, DOI: 10.1080/ 10911359.2014.995392
- Mehta, Deepa. Fire. *Zeitgeist Films*, 1996.
- Monteil, Lucas. "About the Book Terrorist Assemblages: Homonationalism in Queer Times, by Jasbir K. Puar". Durham, NC: Duke University Press, 2007.", Mouvements, vol. 75, no. 3, 2013, pp. 161-165.
- O'Shaughnessy, Haley D. "Homonationalism and the Death of the Radical Queer." *Inquiries Journal/Student Pulse 7.03* (2015). http://www.inquiriesjournal.com/a?id=1003
- *Padmaavat*. Directed by Sanjay Leela Bhansali, performances by Deepika Padukone, Ranveer Singh, and Shahid Kapoor, *Viacom18 Motion Pictures*, 2018.
- Robinson, Brandon Andrew. "Heteronormativity and Homonormativity." *The Wiley Blackwell Encyclopedia of Gender and Sexuality Studies* (2016): 1–3. Web.
- *Sajjan Singh Rangroot*. Pankaj Batra, Diljit Dosanjh, Yograj Singh, Sunanda Sharma, and Jagjeet Sandhu, *Pankaj Batra Films and Vivid Art House*, 2018.
- *Shubh Mangal Zyada Saavdhan*. Directed by Hitesh Kewalya, performances by Ayushmann Khurrana and Jitendra Kumar, *T-Series*, 2020.

- *Waqt: The Race Against Time.* Vipul Amrutlal Shah, Amitabh Bachchan, Akshay Kumar, Priyanka Chopra, Shefali Shah, and Boman Irani, *Blockbuster Movie Entertainers*, 2005.

Padmapriya P., is a PhD Research Scholar in English at SRM Institute of Science and Technology. She worked as an Assistant professor of English in Arts and Science Colleges and earned a total of 5 years and 4 months of teaching experience. She has published five research papers and presented Nine research papers at various conferences and seminars. She has also translated two short stories of the renowned writer Karankarki from Tamil to English.

Dr. A. Ganesan has been serving as an Associate Professor in the Department of English, RKM Vivekananda College, Chennai-04, Tamil Nadu, India. He has cleared both NET and SLET conducted by UNIVERSITY GRANTS COMMISSION and Bharathiar University respectively. He received Ph.D., from AMET University, Chennai. He is the recipient of the Best Paper Award at Annamalai University and United States Cultural Immersion Program Scholarship from the US Government. He has published 26 research papers and 4 handbooks. He is a research supervisor at the University of Madras and guiding 4 scholars presently. He has presented 28 papers at various national and international conferences and has given 38 invited lectures at various universities and colleges. He has completed 7 online courses as well.

• • •

CHAPTER XVII

Retelling Mythos in a Green Light: Exploring the Centrifugal Tendency of Select Mythological Retellings

P. Divya

Assistant Professor, Women's Christian College, Chennai

Abstract

Mythological tales have been in existence since time immemorial, and they not only fascinated human beings with their charms and intrigues, but also influenced their ways of living and inspired their belief systems that remained unshakeable and unquestionable for centuries. However, mythological retellings have often expressed their incredulity to such metanarratives and opened the door for scepticism and subversion. Mythological retellings, in a way, act as a centrifuge as they move away from the centre to focus on the elements that remain on the margins. They seek to include what the centre has hitherto excluded. Mythical retellings namely Kalidasa's *Shakuntala* and Sujata Bhatt's poems titled "A Different Way to Dance" and "What Happened to the Elephant?"have been analysed in this paper in terms of how they strive to be environmentally inclusive by sabotaging the anthropocentric dualities present in dominant mythological tales that act as their source of inspiration. Drawing upon the theories of cultural memory studies, the paper attempts to focus on the notion of environmental memory and its relevance to promoting environmental inclusion in the new epoch of Anthropocene.

Keywords: Mythology, Retellings, Centrifugal tendency, Sabotage, Anthropocentrism, Environmental memory, Cultural memory, Anthropocene.

Mythological tales are attributed a greater level of significance in the domain of cultural studies as they help scholars understand the values and customs of the past thereby allowing them to delineate their implications in the present. Historians often employ myths as tools to study the past not only for analyzing the socio-political structures that existed in different societies across time and space but also for tracing the "history of mentalities" of various social groups which inevitably leads to a better understanding of their collective memory. According to Robert Mandrou, "the history of mentalities aims at reconstructing the patterns of behavior, expressive forms and modes of silence into which worldviews and collective sensibilities are translated" (qtd. in Confino 80). Mythological tales, apart from acting as mediators of cultural memory, also serve as a form of collective memory as they constantly reconstruct the collective sensibilities of the past, which eventually gets re-presented in the present. Mythical tales, therefore, are products of interplay between remembering and forgetting as scholars of cultural memory studies believe that the transmission of cultural memory inevitably involves the act of forgetting.

Mythological tales have often pushed certain elements of the society to the periphery either through the process of "active forgetting" (Assmann 98) or by means of "passive forgetting" (98). However, the forgotten elements are not permanently lost and can be retrieved to promote inclusivity. Literary writers who retell mythical tales are deeply committed to filling the gaps within the canonical texts so as to foreground the significance of peripheral elements that these texts have actively forgotten. Kalidasa's *Shakuntala* is a play that retells an episode from the epic *Mahabharatha* while Sujata Bhatt's "A Different Way to Dance" and

"What Happened to the Elephant?"are poems that narrativise a story from Hindu mythology. Both the retellings shed light on what was marginalized by the canonical mythical texts, i.e., the non-human world and that they are centrifugal in nature as they move away from the centre to infiltrate the peripheral sphere. They not only sabotage anthropocentric attitudes and belief systems, but also challenge the anthropocentric view of the very notion of "memory" itself by providing insight into the concept of environmental memory.

Kalidasa's *Shakuntala* retells the story of the King Dushyanta, which appears in the Adiparva section of the epic *Mahabharata*. Both the epic and its retelling record, the series of events that happened after the romantic encounter between the King Dushyanta of Puru Dynasty and Shakuntala, the adopted daughter of sage Kanva. In the epic, King Dushyanta married Shakuntala in Sage Kanva's hermitage, but subsequently forgot his allegiance to Shakuntala and deliberately refused to recognize her when she appeared along with her son Bharata at Dushyanta's court after six years of their marriage. Dushyantha in Mahabharata deviates from the path of Dharma through his intentional act of forgetting, whereas Kalidasa's Dushyantha continues to uphold his Dharma even in the face of adversity since he does not actively forget Shakuntala, rather the curse incurred by Shakuntala at the hands of sage Durvasa makes it hard for him to recollect the marital bond that he had formed with Sakunthala during his stay at the hermitage. Kalidasa deconstructs the past that was reconstructed by the epic and by doing so, he not only accords the king his due honour but also the natural world its due respect. P.P.Sharma, in his article titled "Kalidasa's Shakuntala: Some Sidelights" says that the epic portrays Dushyanta as a "monstrous slayer" (81) since he kills thousands of wild animals before making his entry in to Sage Kanva's hermitage. Unlike the epic, Kalidasa's Dushyanta, according to Sharma, exhibits a high level of compassion for the non-human world which becomes evident in the first scene of the play where he chooses not to hunt a deer when the hermits plead him to be merciful. While the epic has actively forgotten the natural world, its flora and fauna, Kalidasa's play actively remembers the intrinsic value of various natural elements that inhabit the entire cosmos. Kalidasa's play gives voice and agency to the non-human world which appeared inert and passive in the epic. As P.P.Sharma says, Nature in Kalidasa's play is not merely "a setting or background" (78) and that the playwright has placed "the flora and fauna right at the centre, on par with the significant characters" (78).

While the epic exclusively focuses on the human world in isolation, Kalidasa's play sheds light on the connectedness of the natural world and the human world. In addition, the play also demonstrates the idea that man's dependence upon nature doesn't limit itself to the biological realm, rather it also extends to the sphere of cognition. Environment plays vital role in the sustenance of human memory and in turn, the environmental memory of human beings contributes significantly to the survival of the planet. Jan Assmann, in the article titled "Communicative and Cultural Memory" says that memory depends on communication and social interaction for its development on the social level. While speaking about the significance of Communicative memory, Assmann declares, "Our memory, which we possess as beings equipped with a human mind, exists only in constant interaction not only with other human memories but also with "things," outward symbols" (111). The category of "things" invented by Assmann includes "dishes, feasts, rites, images, stories and other texts, landscapes, and other "lieux de mémoire"" (111). Assmann also adds that these "things" do not have a memory of their own, but they still carry the memories which humans have endowed on them.

Kalidasa's play can be analyzed through the lens of communicative memory to understand the indispensability of the natural world. The description of Kanva's hermitage, offered by the playwright, blurs the distinction between the human world and the natural world as the inhabitants of the grove, including the flora and the fauna, live in close communion with each other through mutual help and constant interaction. The play contains several instances that stand testimony to such a harmonious way of living. In Act 1, Dushyanta refers to Shakuntala and her friends as "Flower-children of the wood" (8) which reveals the familial bonding between the human and the non-human residents of the hermitage. This is further reinforced in the subsequent scene where Shakuntala exhibits her sisterly affection for the flora of the grove while watering trees along with her friends Anusuya and Priyamvada. In addition, the spring-creeper that was planted and cherished by Father Kanva, holds a symbolic significance in Shakuntala's life as it has been described as having the capacity of predicting Shakuntala's future. Moreover, Shakuntala also expresses her admiration for the entanglement of the mango tree and the jasmine-vine which has been nick-named by her as "Light of the Grove". Shakuntala's relationship with the fauna of the grove displays her maternal qualities as she nurses an injured young fawn to recovery. Shakuntala's constant interaction with both the natural and the cultural elements of her immediate surrounding helps in building and sustaining her cultural and ecological memories. These ecological memories, in turn, help Shakuntala and other human inhabitants of the grove establish an inclusive community that accommodates both beings and elements of the natural world as Jan Assmann declares that memory allows us to live in communities and living in communities in turn "enables us to build a memory" (109).

The notion of memory remained within the anthropocentric domain for a long time, but eventually underwent a transition when the scholars of cultural memory studies credited the non-human world with the task of carrying human memories which proves the inevitable need of their presence for the existence of human memory. However, Kalidasa's play foregrounds the memory of the natural world which the dominant discourses on memory have relegated to the periphery. The play exemplifies that the flora and the fauna within the non-human sphere also have a memory of their own, to a certain extent. For instance, When Shakuntala leaves the hermitage in Act.4 for Dushyanta's Kingdom, not only her human companions grieve over her parting, but also the natural world expresses its anguish over the separation of the being who loved them dearly and tended to their needs with utmost care and attention. The peahen, in her sorrowful state, refuses to dance and likewise, the doe stops taking its feed. The young fawn that was adopted by Shakuntala during its miserable times, also remembers her gentle acts of kindness and pulls at her dress, evidently signifying its denial to leave her side.

In another instance, when Father Kanva invokes the trees of the grove to seek their protection for Shakuntala in her journey, he recounts the intimate and empathetic relationship that Shakuntala had with the flora of the hermitage. Shakuntala, according to the sage, never failed to water the trees as she perceived the task as "a sister's duty" and never plucked their flowers since she appreciated their intrinsic values far more than the "selfish beauty". Also, when the trees bore blossoms, she completely rejoiced as how one would celebrate a festival.

The flora of the grove, in turn, bestows Shakuntala with silken dress and the finest ornaments when she bids them farewell, which demonstrates their ability to recollect Shakuntala's courtesy and acts of benevolence. Though these instances contain surrealistic elements, the fact that Kalidasa stresses the need for understanding the natural world is undeniable. The cognitive and emotional capacities of non-human beings, though limited, need to be acknowledged and appreciated for promoting planetary richness and well-being.

Lawrence Buell, in the article titled "Uses and Abuses of Environmental Memory", describes the constructive uses of environmental memory wherein he says that the "environmental memory is a powerful existential reality" (112) and that "the environmental loss often cuts deeper than human loss" (113). Shakuntala's grief during her departure from the hermitage, intensifies because of her environmental memory and she constantly expresses her concern over the changes that the flora and the fauna would possibly undergo during her absence.

Shakuntala reminds her friends and Father Kanva to take good care of the species and expresses her deep sense of agony over their separation from her. However, as Buell says, environmental memory still acts "as energizer, whether to undermine, to liftup", to traumatize" (113).

According to Buell, the third use of environmental memory is that it can negate the autonomy of humans, either at an individual level or of the whole species (113). Such negations would ultimately instil a sense of humility among human beings and help them understand that environmental markers are indispensable to cultural survival. King Dushyanta in Kalidasa's play gains this understanding when he descends from heaven in his chariot after having assisted Lord Indra in waging a war against demonic forces. While flying in the air along with Indra's charioteer Matali, Dushyanta gets an aerial view of the earth, its mountains, plains, streams, flora and fauna which eventually trigger his environmental memory. The King expresses his adoration for the natural world after having received a "clearer view" of the same and in response to the King's admiration, Matali says, "There is a noble loveliness in the earth" (83). This scene demonstrates that environmental memories are essential for the survival of mankind as it annihilates their inner ego and offers them a sense of belonging.

While Kalidasa's play illustrates the uses of environmental memory, Sujata Bhatt's poem, "What Happened to the Elephant?"undermines the abuses of environmental memory. The poem "What Happened to the Elephant?"is a sequel to another poem titled "A Different Way to Dance"that revolves around the story of the Lord Ganesh from Hindu mythology. Lord Ganesh is usually referred to as "Gajapati" or "the elephant headed" in Hindu mythology as his head had been replaced with that of an elephant after Lord Shiva decapitated Ganesh's head in a fit of anger. Sujata Bhatt's poems reconstruct the past in a green light, so as to narrate the story of the non-human world that the dominant myth has failed to include and such retellings have the potential to disrupt not only the age-old myth but also the collective memory of people that it engendered.

Lawrence Buell, in his discussion on abuses of memory, offers a list of memory dysfunctions put forth by psychologist Daniel Schacter under the label "the seven sins of memory" (105). The mythical tale that the poems of Bhatt undermine exhibit two of these dysfunctions, namely, misattribution and bias. The myth has not only misattributed the non-human world with the sole purpose of serving its creators but also prioritizes the interests of the creators, without having any consideration for the needs and the desires of the created, i.e., the non-human species. Consequently, it implies the idea that non-human species should extend their stewardship to the beings in power, even at the cost of giving up on their own lives. The poem "A Different Way to Dance"challenges this lopsided view of the myth through the process of giving voice to the elephant whose story remained forgotten for several centuries. The poem expresses the elephant's intense longing for the life that it once lived and the sensory perceptions that it has had in its own habitat.

The sequel to the above-mentioned poem, "What Happened to the Elephant?" echoes the concerns of a child, who after having listened to the story, questions the narrator about the fate of the elephant that was beheaded. Through this poem, Bhatt foregrounds the idea that the story of the elephant needs to be told as it contributes a great deal to building the environmental memory of the child and also has the potential to transform the child into an agent of change and an environmentally conscious being.

Rosanne Kennedy, in the article titled, "Multidirctional Eco-Memory in an Era of Extinction" explains his conception of eco-memory and multidirectional eco-memory. Kennedy perceives eco-memory as "grounded in a deep memory of a habitat, conceived as an ecological assemblage in which all elements, human and nonhuman, are mobile, connected, and interactive" (269). Bhatt's poem can be analyzed using the lens of Multidirectional Eco-memory. The child in the poem ponders over the possibility of replacing the head of the elephant with that of a horse in order to revive the elephants's body. However, the child also contemplates the predicament of the horse after it loses its head to save the elephant. The poem clearly illustrates the notion of an ecological assemblage where a minor disturbance at a particular point can collapse the entire assemblage. Therefore, the exclusion of the non-human world in collective memory inevitably excludes human beings as human memories cannot exist in isolation. Bhatt's poems effectively configure the idea that environmental memories are intricately bound to cultural memories.

Memories play a significant role in influencing our perception of the world and by means of reconstructing the past, they allow us to shape our future. Though memories are not entirely reliable as they dysfunction in several ways, what they construct and carry forward have profound social, political and cultural implications. Mythical tales build cultural and collective memories as they have often transported the mentalities of societies from the past to the present. These collective memories can shape the memories of an individual and vice versa. When environmental memories are excluded from such collective memories, they not only affect the non-human world but also the human beings whose lives are embedded in a broader ecological network. Mythical retellings like Kalidasa's *Shakuntala* and Sujata Bhatt's poems seek to promote inclusivity as they shed light on the marginal elements and bring them to the forefront. Eco-memory or Environmental memory is one such marginal element in the domain of memory studies. The primary texts chosen for this study impart us with a deeper sense of knowledge about environmental memory. The environment builds and acts as carriers of human memory. Environmental memory of human beings, in turn, contribute to the flourishing of the non-human world. The study demonstrates the fact that the symbiotic relationship between human beings and the natural world works even at cognitive level and cognitive symbiosis would ensure the sustenance and the survival of both the parties involved.

References

- Assmann, Jan. "Communicative and Cultural Memory." *Cultural Memory Studies an International and Interdisciplinary Handbook*, by Astrid Erll et al., Walter De Gruyter, Berlin, 2008, pp. 109-118.
- Bhatt, Sujata. "A Different Way to Dance", "What Happened to the Elephant?." *Collected Poems*, Carcanet Press Ltd, 2013
- Buell, Lawrence. "Uses and Abuses of Environmental Memory." *Contesting Environmental Imaginaries: Nature and Counternature in a Time of Global Change*, by Steven P. Hartman, Brill, Leiden, 2017, pp. 93-116.
- Confino, Alon. "Memory and the History of Mentalities." *Cultural Memory Studies: An International and Interdisciplinary Handbook*, by Astrid Erll et al., Walter De Gruyter, Berlin, 2008, pp. 77–84.
- Kalidasa. *Shakuntala.* Translated by Arthur W. Ryder, In parentheses Publications, 1999.
- Kennedy, Rosanne. "Multidirectional Eco-Memory in an Era of Extinction: Colonial Whaling and Indigenous Dispossession in Kim Scott's That Deadman Dance." *The Routledge Companion to the Environmental Humanities*, by Ursula K. Heise et al., Routledge, New York, 2021, pp. 268–277.
- Sharma, P. P. "Kalidasa's Shakuntala: Some Sidelights." *Indian Literature*, vol. 22, no. 3, 1979, pp. 75–85. *JSTOR*, http://www.jstor.org/stable/23329988. Accessed 4 Jan. 2023.

P. Divya, is Assistant Professor of English at Women's Christian College, Chennai. Her broad areas of interest include environmental humanities and medical humanities. She is committed to the task of studying and teaching emerging fields of study within the domain of literature. As a dedicated researcher, she seeks to explore the unexplored so as to experience several moments of epiphany.

• • •

CHAPTER XVIII

Inclusivity of Modernity in diverse Tribal Culture as Reflected in the Novel The Stupid Cupid by Mamang Dai

Preha C.[1] and Dr. Crispine Shiny[2]

[1]Research Scholar, Department of English, Karunya Institute of Technology and Sciences, Coimbatore, 641114

[2]Assistant Professor, Department of English, Karunya Institute of Technology and Sciences, Coimbatore, 641114

Abstract

This article focuses on the major aspects of inclusivity of the modern culture into the diverse culture of tribes. The change in socio-cultural aspects of tribal culture is reflected in the novel *Stupid Cupid*. Dai bring out many tribal women characters who broke their cultural barriers by educating themselves and migrating towards city to lead an independent life. The characters Adna and Mareb break the traditional beliefs of their native places where cross-cultural marriages are not allowed. They both fell in love with non-tribal men from Delhi which breaks all of their cultural stereotypes. Adna also introduces the tribal culture into the city life. She constructed her late aunt's apartment in the city as a meeting place for lovers and friends. It is a common practice of certain group of tribes to spend some time together in a particular place. The breaking of traditional barriers of tribes by the inclusivity of modern culture made many significant changes in the entire tribal community for their upliftment. To elaborate this concept of inclusivity, the theory of Cross-culture can be adopted in which interaction between different culture and its impacts were analyzed.

Key Words: Inclusivity, Modernity, Cultural transformation, Cultural diversity, Cross Culture

---

Introduction

Tribes are the most ethnic group of Indian society. They live in forests and slopes of mountains; they usually isolate themselves from other community people to protect their land, people, and culture. Their culture is unique and differs from mainstream cultural practices significantly. The tribal people express their cultural identity and distinctiveness in their social and political organizations, language, festivals, and rituals as well as in their ornaments, dress, technology, art, and craft. The tribal culture of India has undergone changes owing to several factors, such as impact of education introduced by government or missionaries, advancement of communication, industrialization, and urbanization. The major reason for industrialization has been that the tribal area is very rich in mineral and other natural resources throughout the country. This paper discuss about the inclusivity of modernity in tribal culture for adapting themselves to the changing lifestyle of the outer world. It provides equal access to opportunities and resources for people who might otherwise be excluded or marginalized. Modernity refers to the ways of life, attitudes and values that are associated with the present time and the current era. Inclusivity in modernity means that all groups and individuals within a society have equal access and opportunities to participate in the benefits and practices of modernity.

In this context of different tribal cultures, inclusivity in modernity can be a complex and sensitive issue. On one hand, modernity can bring many benefits to tribal cultures, such as access to education, healthcare, and technology. On the other hand, the process of modernization can also lead to the loss of traditional cultural practices and values and can result in the marginalization and displacement of indigenous peoples.

It is important to approach the relationship between tribal cultures and modernity with sensitivity and respect for the unique histories, traditions and values of each culture. It is also important to recognize the rights of tribes to maintain their cultural identities and practices, and to ensure that they have a meaningful say in decisions which affect their lives and communities.

About the author

Mamang Dai was born on February 23, 1957 at Pasighat, East Siang district, to Matin Dai and Odi Dai. She belongs to the Adi tribe. She did her schooling in Pine Mount School, Shillong, and Meghalaya. She finished her Bachelor in English literature from Gauhati University, Assam. In 1979, She was selected in the IAS exam, but she resigned the post to pursue her dream job of journalism. She is the first woman to be selected for IAS from her state. While working as a journalist, she contributed to various journals like The Telegraph, Hindustan Times and *The Sentinel*. She also worked in TV-AIR and DDK, Itanagar as well as in the radio, where she worked as an anchor and conducted many interviews. She was appointed as a programme officer at Worldwide Fund for Nature, known as WWF, where she worked in the Eastern Himalayas Biodiversity Hotspots programme. She was the former secretary of Press Club in Itanagar. She was the president of Arunachal Pradesh Union of Working Journalists (APUW). She was appointed as a member of Arunachal Pradesh state public service commission in 2011. Her non-fictional works are *Arunachal Pradesh: The Hidden Land* (2003) and *Dairy farming: The Food of Arunachal* (2004). *The Sky Queen and Once Upon a Moon time* (2003) are illustrated folklore texts. She published *The Legends of Pensam* as her first novel in 2006, which was followed by *Stupid Cupid* (2008) and *The Black Hill* (2014) *Escaping the Land* (2021). *River Poems* (2004), *The Balm of Time* (2008), *Midsummer Survival Lyrics* (2014), *Hambreelmai's Loom* (2014) are her poetry collections. *The Balm of Time* was also published in Assamese as *El Balsamo Del YTiempo*. When she began writing, she wrote romantic verse and stories.

She then changed from the theme of the self to focus on a larger reality. She reflects upon the sense of a close knit community living in remote places. Some of the important positions that she has occupied comprise General Secretary of the Literary Society in Arunachal Pradesh, member of the North East Writers' Forum and General Council member of the Sahitya and Sangeet Natak Akademi. In 2011, She received Padma Shri from the Government of India. In 2013, the government of Arunachal Pradesh conferred on her annual Verrier Elwin Prize for her book *Arunachal Pradesh: The Hidden Land*. In 2017, She received Sahitya Akademi Award for her novel *The Black Hill*.

Cross Culture

Cross-cultural theory is a theoretical framework that seeks to understand and explain how cultural differences can shape and influence various aspects of human behavior and character. This includes understanding how cultural values, beliefs, and practices can shape attitudes, communication styles, social norms, and other important aspects of human behavior.

One of the key components of cross-cultural theory is the concept of cultural relativism, which asserts that the values and behaviors of a given culture should be understood and evaluated within the context of that culture, rather than being judged based on the values and norms of another culture. This means that what may be considered acceptable or appropriate behavior in one culture may not be in another, and it is important to understand and appreciate the cultural differences that shape the way people think and behave.

Other important concepts in cross-cultural theory include the role of power dynamics in shaping cultural interactions, the importance of understanding and addressing cultural bias, and the impact of globalization on cultural exchange and integration. Overall, cross-cultural theory is an important concept for anyone seeking to understand and navigate the complexities of cultural differences, whether in personal relationships, business, or other areas of life.

In tribal cultures, cross-cultural theory can be seen particularly relevant because tribes often have distinct cultural practices and traditions that may differ significantly from those of mainstream society. These cultural differences can have a significant impact on how tribal members interact with one another and with people from other cultures. For example, some tribal cultures place a strong emphasis on community and collectivism, while others may value individualism and autonomy. These differences can affect how tribal members make decisions, solve problems, and relate to one another. By understanding these differences, individuals and organizations can better navigate cross-cultural interactions and communications with tribal cultures. This can help to build stronger relationships and promote mutual understanding and respect.

Modernity in tribal culture

Modernity has a significant impact on cultural changes. It has led to the rise of secularism and the decline of traditional religious and cultural practices. It also brought about the idea of individualism and self-expression, as well as new forms of art and literature that reflected the changing world.

In addition, modernity has led to the emergence of new forms of communication, such as the Internet, which has made it easier to share information and ideas globally. This has led to the rise of a global culture and the blurring of traditional cultural boundaries. Moreover, modernity has also led to changes in the way we live and work, with people becoming more self-centric and living in urban areas has change in their mindset. This has led to the rise of multicultural societies, where people from different backgrounds live and work together. This has brought about new challenges and opportunities for integration and understanding.

In a gist, modernity has brought about significant cultural changes that has shaped the world as it is today, challenging traditional values and practices, creating new forms of art and literature, facilitating the rise of a global culture and multicultural societies and leading to the changes in the way we live and work.

Modernization can have a wide-ranging impact on different fields of tribal culture, including economy, education, healthcare, social and political systems which as follows:

Economy: Modernization can bring economic benefits to tribal cultures, such as increased access to markets and resources, improved infrastructure, and new opportunities for income generation. However, it can also lead to the displacement of traditional livelihoods, such as hunting and gathering flower, farming, and fishing, and the erosion of traditional land rights.

Education: Modernization can lead to increased access to education for tribal people, which can help to improve literacy rates, increase understanding of different cultures and ways of life, and promote inclusivity and tolerance. However, it can also lead to the erosion of traditional knowledge and practices, and a lack of respect for the unique cultural heritage of tribal people.

Healthcare: Modernization can improve access to healthcare and medical services for tribal people, which can help to improve health outcomes and reduce mortality rates. However, modernization can also lead to the erosion of traditional healing practices.

Social and Political Systems: Modernization has lead to the introduction of new social and political systems, such as democracy and human rights, which has helped to promote greater equality and participation in decision-making processes. However, it has also lead to the erosion of traditional social systems and a lack of respect for the unique cultural heritage of tribal people. It's important to note that these impacts can vary depending on the specific context and the particular cultural tribe. Therefore, it's important to approach modernization in a culturally sensitive way and to take into account the unique needs and perspectives of tribal communities.

Tribal culture in Arunachal Pradesh

Arunachal Pradesh is a state in Northeastern India. It is a home to many different tribal communities. Some of the major tribes in Arunachal Pradesh include the Adi, Apatani, Nyishi, Monpa, and Sherdukpen. Each of these tribes has its own unique culture, language, and traditions. The state is known for its rich diversity of tribal cultures and languages, with more than 50 different tribal languages spoken in the state. The tribes in Arunachal Pradesh have a long history of living in harmony with their environment and have developed a deep respect for nature. Many of the tribal communities in the state depend on agriculture and forestry for their livelihoods and have a strong tradition of conservation.

The Adi tribe is a large indigenous group who are believed to be descendants of the ancient Tibeto- Burman people and have a unique culture and way of life. The Adi language belongs to the Tani group of Tibeto- Burman languages and is spoken by around 330,000 people. The Adi people follow a traditional religion known as Donyi-Polo, which is based on the worship of the sun and the moon. They also follow animistic beliefs and practices.

The Adi people have a rich tradition of folk music, dance, and storytelling, and their handicrafts are highly prized. They are known for their hand-woven shawls, carpets, and baskets, as well as their woodcarving and blacksmithing skills. The Adi people have a matrilineal system of inheritance, in which property and wealth are passed down through the female line.

Agriculture is the main source of livelihood for the Adi people, and they grow a variety of crops, including rice, maize, millet, and beans. The Adi people have a strong sense of community and participate in traditional festivals and ceremonies that are an important part of their culture.

Cultural changes in *The Stupid Cupid*

The change in socio-cultural aspects of tribal culture is reflected in the novel *Stupid Cupid*. In this novel, Dai introduced many tribal women characters who broke their cultural barriers by educating themselves and migrating towards city to lead an independent life. They enjoy freedom to take their own decision of life without the support of other gender. Adna says that she liked everything about Delhi. She says:

... this anonymity was the very thing I liked. After the watchful expectations of a small town, being a total stranger among strangers was a relief and a pleasure... I like the heavy evenings, filled with diesel fumes and smoke, and the heat burning our faces ... dusty trees in full bloom...Coming out of restaurants we would stand under the trees and puff at our cigarettes. It was all very different from where I came (Dai 2009, p.14).

The characters Adna and Mareb break the traditional beliefs of their native places where cross-cultural marriages were not allowed. They both fell in love with non-tribal men from Delhi. Even her aunt married non-tribal man which breaks all of their cultural stereotypes. This novel also depicts the condition of migrated women who faces severe racial discrimination by the city dwellers. It went to an extreme with the murder of Adna's closest friend Amine for money. On the other hand, the condition of tribal women in their native land is pathetic and it is also portrayed in this novel. Mareb's mother sacrifices herself in the attempt of being the perfect homemaker. Mareb recalls how her mother looked after the house by "obeying the instructions of her father". The narrator of the novel, Adna describes how Mareb recalls her mother. All Mareb remembered of her was her putting up curtains, sewing lace on to the borders of tablecloths and providing some semblance of grace and good living in a life that was constantly on the move ... (Dai 2009, 37). Moreover, these societies is a patriarchal societies and women are still ignored. Restrictions are made on women's access to knowledge and it is men who are the decision makers in both public and private affairs, in most of the tribal communities of Northeast.

The exploitation of natural resources from indigenous or tribal communities has been a widespread issue throughout history. As societies have industrialized and modernized, many governments and corporations have sought to extract resources such as minerals, timber, and oil from lands traditionally inhabited by indigenous peoples. These actions have often been done without consent or compensation, and have led to the displacement of communities, destruction of the environment, and the loss of traditional ways of life. This exploitation has also been linked to human rights violations, including forced evictions, violence, and discrimination.

...Assam was rich in oil and tea, and they said it was all being taken away from the people to whom it really belonged. We are fighting for a fair deal,' they cried. We did not know what ramifications would follow, but at the time we were well aware that the 'Agitation', as it was called, was inviting a great deal of media attention, and that the Centre was taking notice. (Dai 2009, p.13).

Conclusion

The tribes are subjected to the forces of change, both indigenous and exogenous; consequently, they have serious ramifications on their lifestyle and culture and cross their cultural boundaries in order to adapt to the changing lifestyle of the modern world. This process got further affected by the induction of the act of globalization which brought a homogeneous consumerist culture and value system into society. The resulting changes in the characters of the tribes further endorsed the fading vigor and vitality of the tribal culture. The adaptation of modernity in tribal culture can be a complex and nuanced process. On one hand, modernity can bring about positive changes for tribal communities, such as improved access to education, healthcare, and economic opportunities. It can also lead to the preservation and revitalization of traditional cultures and practices through the use of new technologies and forms of communication.

On the other hand, the process of modernization can also have negative effects on tribal cultures. The rapid pace of change can lead to the erosion of traditional values and practices, and the loss of traditional knowledge and ways of life. Additionally, the introduction of market-based economies and the commodification of traditional goods and practices can lead to the exploitation of tribal communities.

For some tribes, the adaptation of modernity can be a slow and gradual process, while for others it can happen more rapidly. Some tribes may choose to adapt to modernity on the other hand it preserves their traditional culture and values, while others may be forced to adapt due to external pressures.

It's important to note that the relationship between tribal culture and modernity can be complex and dynamic, and it's important to approach the topic with sensitivity, respect and understanding. It's important to support the preservation of traditional culture and knowledge and respect the autonomy of tribal communities in choosing how to adapt to modernity.

Overall, the adaptation of modernity in tribal culture can bring about both positive and negative effects, and it's important to approach the topic with sensitivity and respect for the autonomy of tribal communities.

References

- Dai, Mamang. *"Stupid Cupid"*. Penguin.2009.
- Esther Daimari. "Images of women in Mamang Dai's Fiction." New Academia. Vol. II, Oct 2013. https://en.wikipedia.org/wiki/Adi_people.Accessed 15 Nov 2022.
- Mamang Dai. Wikiwand. https://www.wikiwand.com/en/Mamang_Dai. Accessed 15 Nov 2022.
- Padmavathi. M.*"Acculturization and changing attitude towards the tribal community in Andhra Pradesh"*.Jetir. June 2019. https://www.jetir.org/papers/JETIR1908982.pdf.Accessed 15 Nov 2022.
- PunthiPustak, Calcutta, 1986. http://ignca.gov.in/Asi_data/74294.pdf. Accessed 15 Nov 2022.
- Verma, Vineet Kumar.*"Tribal Culture of India: General and Specific Characteristics of Tribes"*. Athshala. May 2013.

https://epgp.inflibnet.ac.in/epgpdata/uploads/epgp_content /S000001AN/P001118/M013296/ET/14634755502et.pdf. Accessed 15 Nov 2022.

- Vidyarthi. L. P; Singh K, Ajit. *"The Bio-cultural profiles of tribal Bihar"*. https://www.indian culture.gov.in/ebooks/bio-cultural-profiles-tribal-bihar. Accessed 15 Nov 2022.
- "Cultural   transformationtheory". wikipedia.https://en.wikipedia.org/wiki/Cultural _transformation _theory.Accessed15 Nov2022.

---

[1]Preha C., is a research scholar at Karunya Institute of Technology and Sciences in Coimbatore, with a particular focus on tribal literature. She obtained her Bachelor's degree from PSGRKrishnammal College for Women in Coimbatore and her Master's degree from Women's Christian College in Nagercoil. Preha is committed to exploring the intricacies of tribal literature and comprehending the cultural and social challenges that tribal communities encounter. Her research has been presented at both national and international conferences, highlighting her academic contributions. Preha's passion for literature and social justice is evident in her scholarly pursuits and her contributions to the research field.

[2]Dr. Crispine Shiny, is an accomplished assistant professor at Karunya University. She completed her MA, M.Phil, and PhD degrees at Karunya University, establishing a strong foundation in her area of expertise. Dr. Crispine Shiny has an impressive research record, having published multiple papers in Scopus-indexed journals and presented her research at numerous national and international conferences. Her scholarly contributions have earned her recognition and respect within the academic community. As an assistant professor, Dr. Crispine Shiny is dedicated to advancing the field of English language and literature and making valuable contributions to the academic community.

CHAPTER XIX

Spatial and Ethnic Inclusiveness in Gothic Setting: A study in The Silence of the Ghosts by Jonathan Aycliffe and That Frequent Visitor by Hari Kumar

Ramya B.[1] and Dr. Poonam[2]

[1]*Research Scholar, Department of EFL, SRM IST*

[2]*Assistant Professor, Research Supervisor, Department of EFL, SRM IST*

Abstract

Ghost stories are a sign that symbolizes their existence and is shrouded in mystery. The term "spatial inclusiveness" relates to the location in gothic fiction entrenched in cultural tradition. The enigma's physical incarnation is a gothic setting. The gothic settings are various, such as Ancestral properties, isolated houses, a spooky castle, incomplete construction, and a graveyard. Inheriting family property is typical, although such land frequently becomes mysterious. This article investigates the ethnic inclusion of the representations of family property in *The Silence of the Ghosts* by Jonathan Aycliffe and *That Frequent Visitor* by Hari Kumar. Gothic narratives generally focus on a single location, typically a house haunted by a malevolent force that intends to harm its inhabitants. This paper emphasizes the ancestral property as a gothic setting that embodies ethnic inclusivity in gothic spatial inclusiveness.

Further, the study focuses on the portrayal of ancestral property, how it connects to the people, and how the space hides and reveals the truth behind the mystery.

Keywords: Spatial inclusiveness, ethnic inclusivity, ancestral property, gothic setting and mystery

---

Gothic Fiction

Gothic fiction can also be seen as a response to Enlightenment ideas, which emphasized reason and science over superstition and the supernatural. Gothic fiction often incorporates supernatural elements that challenge Enlightenment ideas and reflects a growing fascination with the dark and mysterious, as well as a desire to explore the irrational and the subconscious. The use of supernatural elements in Gothic fiction settings contributes to the genre's themes and motifs by creating an atmosphere of fear, mystery, and uncertainty. Supernatural elements, such as ghosts, monsters, or supernatural powers, serve to heighten the sense of danger and challenge the characters' understanding of the world around them. This contributes to the central themes of the genre, such as the struggle between good and evil, the exploration of human fears and desires, and the confrontation of the unknown.

In addition, the use of supernatural elements allows Gothic fiction to delve into philosophical and psychological themes, such as the nature of reality, the power of the imagination, and the human condition. By incorporating supernatural elements into the setting, Gothic fiction can explore these themes in a more imaginative and symbolic way, adding layers of meaning and complexity to the genre.

In this way, the use of supernatural elements in Gothic fiction settings is central to the genre's ability to create a unique and compelling atmosphere, and to explore deep and complex themes that are unique to the Gothic tradition.

Gothic Setting

The setting is paramount in gothic fiction, and contemporary authors are challenged to create vibrant worlds without indulging in lengthy, tedious descriptions of their landscapes. The settings in Gothic fiction often reflect the social, cultural, and historical changes of the time in which they were written. Gothic fiction emerged in the late 18th century and was popular in the late 19th and early 20th centuries. During this time, there was a growing sense of uncertainty and change in Europe, with rapid industrialization and urbanization leading to major social and cultural shifts. This is reflected in the Gothic fiction of the time, which often takes place in dark and decaying environments, reflecting the sense of unease and fear that characterized the period.

The setting in Gothic fiction is characterized by an atmosphere of mystery, fear, and suspense, with a focus on dark, brooding, and often haunted or decaying locations. This creates a mood of foreboding and unease, which is further emphasized by the use of supernatural elements, such as ghosts, monsters, or other supernatural beings. The tone of Gothic fiction is typically gloomy and macabre, with an emphasis on the darker aspects of human nature and the human experience. In contrast, other literary genres, such as romance or comedy, may have a lighter, more upbeat atmosphere and tone, and may focus on more optimistic themes and motifs.

Gothic fiction settings can contribute to the genre's efforts to create a more inclusive and diverse cultural landscape. By increasing representation and visibility, fostering empathy, raising awareness, and breaking stereotypes, Gothic fiction can play an important role in promoting a more nuanced and representative understanding of the experiences and perspectives of marginalized communities.

Common elements in Gothic fiction are Haunted Castles or Mansions that often feature haunted or decaying castles or mansions that serve as the main setting and symbolize the dark and mysterious elements of the genre. Isolation often takes place in remote or isolated locations, such as a small town or a remote island, to heighten the feeling of unease and to limit the characters' escape routes. Decay and Desolation are often depicted as being in a state of decay, with ruined buildings and abandoned landscapes, creating an eerie and unsettling atmosphere. The inclusion of diverse and inclusive settings can introduce new themes and motifs, such as identity, representation, and social justice. The inclusion of diverse and inclusive settings in Gothic fiction can reflect the growing recognition of social justice issues and the importance of representation and representation. The portrayal of marginalized communities and spaces can provide a backdrop for exploring themes related to identity, representation, and social justice, highlighting the issues faced by these communities and promoting empathy and understanding.

The inclusion of diverse and inclusive settings can challenge traditional representations and subvert dominant narratives by providing new perspectives and experiences that differ from the traditional representation. This can provide a more complex and nuanced understanding of the genre's themes and motifs. Gothic fiction often employs foreshadowing to create a sense of unease and suspense, hinting at future events or supernatural occurrences before they happen. Gothic fiction uses a dark and gloomy atmosphere to create a feeling of fear and unease. This is achieved through the use of vivid and evocative descriptions of the setting, as well as the incorporation of supernatural elements. It is characterized by its dark and eerie atmosphere, which is often created through the use of isolated and remote settings. The isolation of traditional Gothic fiction settings, such as castles, monasteries, and manors, creates a feeling of detachment and detachment from the outside world, contributing to the genre's themes of fear and isolation. The isolation and detachment from the outside world create a sense of mystery and unpredictability, contributing to the genre's themes of fear and unease.

Gothic fiction often uses symbols and motifs, such as ruins, skeletons, and bats, to create a sense of fear and to hint at deeper meanings. The setting in Gothic fiction can also serve as a symbolic backdrop to the story. The dark and eerie atmosphere can represent the characters' internal struggles, while the supernatural elements can represent the irrational and unknown aspects of the human experience. The setting can provide obstacles and challenges for the characters, drive the plot forward, and serve as a backdrop for deeper symbolic meaning. It often features characters who are struggling with fear, guilt, or other psychological traumas, which contributes to the unsettling atmosphere of the genre. The exclusionary nature of traditional Gothic fiction settings is often used to create a sense of danger and tension. Characters in Gothic fiction are often isolated from the outside world and must navigate the dangers and mysteries of the setting, contributing to the genre's themes of fear and isolation. Gothic fiction often takes place in historical settings, such as castles, monasteries, or ancient ruins, while slasher and supernatural horror often take place in contemporary settings, such as urban environments or suburbs. Gothic fiction is characterized by its use of supernatural elements, such as ghosts, vampires, and supernatural forces, while slasher and supernatural horror often feature more physical threats, such as serial killers or demonic entities. It explores deeper themes related to human existence and spirituality, while slasher and supernatural horror may focus more on visceral thrills and scares. It is known for its ornate and complex style, while slasher and supernatural horror often have a more straightforward and suspenseful style.

The settings in Indian and British Gothic fiction reflect the attitudes and beliefs about death, the supernatural, and the afterlife in the respective cultures by incorporating local legends, folklore, and cultural myths. These cultural elements shape the depiction of the supernatural in the settings, and the genre's themes about death, fear, and the unknown. For example, in Indian Gothic fiction, the supernatural elements often draw on Hinduism and traditional Indian beliefs about reincarnation, ghosts, and spirits, while in British Gothic fiction, these elements are often rooted in Christianity and Western beliefs about the afterlife. The changing attitudes and beliefs about death and the supernatural in each culture can be seen in the evolution of the genre, with Indian Gothic fiction becoming increasingly influenced by postcolonial and independence-era cultural and political developments.

The isolated haunted property setting in Gothic fiction often contributes to the genre's themes of fear, mystery, and the unknown by creating a sense of isolation and confinement. The remote location of the property adds to the sense of danger and the unknown, as it is removed from the safety and familiarity of civilization. This setting also adds to the mystery of the story, as the isolation often allows for hidden secrets and unknown histories to be revealed. The haunting or supernatural elements of the property add to the fear factor and the unknown, as they challenge the characters' sense of reality and security. Overall, the isolated haunted property setting in Gothic fiction enhances the genre's exploration of fear, mystery, and the unknown by creating a sense of dread and uncertainty.

The choice of setting in Indian and British Gothic fiction reflects the cultural, historical, and social differences between the two countries to a significant extent. Indian Gothic fiction often draws on the country's rich cultural heritage, including Hindu and Muslim myths and legends, as well as its colonial and postcolonial history. This leads to the depiction of unique and distinctive haunted properties and settings that reflect India's cultural and historical context. On the other hand, British Gothic fiction is often set in isolated and decaying estates and castles, reflecting the country's history and cultural obsession with the genteel and the grandiose. These settings often reflect the anxieties and fears of British society during the time in which the works were written. As a result, the choice of setting in both Indian and British Gothic fiction serves as a reflection of the cultural, historical, and social differences between the two countries, contributing to the genre's cultural significance and evolution.

Ethnic Inclusivity in Gothic Spatial Inclusiveness

Spatial inclusiveness in Gothic refers to the effort to create an environment in Gothic architecture and related spaces that is welcoming and accessible to a diverse range of people, regardless of their background or identity. This includes ensuring that people with disabilities, different gender identities, sexual orientations, ages, cultures, and ethnicities feel comfortable and safe in these spaces. The concept of spatial inclusiveness is important in Gothic architecture and related spaces, as these settings are often associated with exclusivity, darkness, and mystery. Gothic spaces can evoke strong emotions and have a significant impact on the well-being of visitors. By promoting spatial inclusiveness, Gothic architecture and related spaces can become more welcoming and inclusive, fostering a sense of community and belonging among diverse groups of people.

Ethnic inclusivity refers to the intentional effort to create an environment where people from diverse ethnic and cultural backgrounds feel welcome, respected, and valued. It involves ensuring that individuals and groups from different ethnicities are not discriminated against or excluded based on their background but instead have equal access to opportunities and resources. The concept of ethnic inclusivity recognizes the unique experiences, perspectives, and contributions of people from different ethnicities and seeks to promote diversity, equity, and inclusion. It is an important aspect of creating a more just and equitable society and fostering a sense of belonging for all individuals.

Ancestral property as a Gothic setting refers to the use of inherited properties or family estates with a dark and mysterious history as a backdrop for Gothic literature or media. Such settings often evoke a sense of foreboding and unease, with the architecture and decor of the property reflecting the wealth and power of the previous generations while also hinting at the possibility of hidden secrets, curses, or supernatural forces at work. The use of ancestral properties as a Gothic setting can be traced back to early Gothic literature, where crumbling castles and abandoned mansions were frequently used as settings for horror and suspenseful stories. In modern media, the use of ancestral properties as Gothic settings continues to captivate audiences, with films, TV shows, and novels using these locations to explore themes such as the weight of family legacy, the corruption of power, and the persistence of the past.

"The Silence of the Ghosts" is a British novel by Jonathan Aycliffe that was published in 2016. The story revolves around a young woman named Rachel Ellwood, who inherits a remote farmhouse from her estranged grandfather. She discovers that the house holds a dark history and that the ghostly presence of her ancestors still lingers. "That Frequent Visitor" is an Indian novel by Hari Kumar. K that was published in 2015. The story revolves around Vypeen island where women are not allowed after sunset. It speaks about the happening during the pournami nights. In both novels, the common setting is their ancestral property.

References

- Aycliffe, Jonathan. *The Silence of Ghosts.* Skyhorse, 10 Feb. 2015.
- Daly, Sathyabhama. "Gothic Spaces and the Tropical City: Reading the Crocodile Fury, Haunting the Tiger, Life's Mysteries." *ETropic: Electronic Journal of Studies in the Tropics,* vol. 17, no. 2, 4 Sept. 2018, https://doi.org/10.25120/etropic.17.2.2018.3653. Accessed 28 Mar. 2020.
- Hari Kumar. *That Frequent Visitor : Every Face Has a Darker Side.* New Delhi, Srishti Publishing & Distributors, 2015.
- PRIHODKO, Ganna, et al. "Emotions of Mystery in Gothic Novels and Thrillers." *WISDOM,* vol. 17, no. 1, 21 Mar. 2021, pp. 193–203, https://doi.org/10.24234/wisdom.v17i1.430. Accessed 21 Nov. 2022.

---

[1]**B. Ramya,** received an M. Phil degree in English Literature from the University of Madras, Chennai, India. In 2015 she qualified for NTA NET. She is currently pursuing PhD degree at SRM Institute of Science and Technology, Kattankulathur, India. Her research interests include Semiotics, Culture Studies, and Memory studies.

[2]**Dr. Poonam,** is a UGC NET-qualified Assistant Professor working at SRM Institute of Science and Technology, Kattankulathur, India. Her area of specialization includes Culture Studies, Semiotics, Feminism, Psychoanalysis, Partition studies and

American Literature. She has published papers on the same in highly reputed journals.

•••

196

Deconstructing the gender bias in Amish Tripathi's Ram: The Scion of Ikshvaku and Sita: Warrior of Mithila

R. Lavanya[1] and Dr. K. Muthurajan[2]

[1]*Assistant Professor & Head, Department of English (SF), VHNSN College (Autonomous), Virudhunagar – Tamilnadu*

[2]*Associate Professor of English, Department of English, VHNSN College (Autonomous), Virudhunagar – Tamilnadu*

Abstract

Indian myths are known for its didactic preaching and divinity in it. These mythical stories have been passed through various generations either orally or in written forms. Conveying moral ideas in the form of stories makes an ever-lasting impact in listener's mind. Ancient epics are not just stories, it has the capacity to instil virtues in reader's mind. Gender inclusivity in language plays a vital role in shaping the narrative style of literary genres. The narrative style which deconstructs the gender-bias has a wide reach among the reading public. Modern myth has broken all these conventional style by creating room for the budding writers to explore the bygone familiar themes with unique perception. Amish Tripathi has implemented this concept in his narrative technique, as it enabled him to deconstruct the stereotyped mythical elements. In this paper, I have chosen the first two parts in Ram Chandra Series, "RAM: Scion of Ikshvaku" and "SITA: Warrior of Mithila." Amish Tripathi has defamiliarized the androcentric theory by utilising the gender inclusivity in his narrative style. I have juxtaposed the blended vision of Ram and Sita by deconstructing the divine myth and I have also substantiated my views by listing out unpredictable twists in Amish Tripathi's "Ram Chandra Series."

Key words: Gender inclusivity, demythologization, mythical elements.

Indian myths are known for their didactic preaching and divinity. These mythical stories have been passed through various generations either orally or in written forms. Conveying moral ideas in the form of stories make an ever-lasting impact in the listener's mind.

Ancient epics are not just stories, but they also have the capacity to instil virtues in the reader's mind. Gender inclusivity in language plays a vital role in shaping the narrative style of literary genres. The narrative style which deconstructs the gender-bias has a wide reach among the reading public.

Modern myth has broken all these conventional styles by creating room for the budding writers to explore the bygone familiar themes with unique perception. Amish Tripathi has implemented this concept in his narrative technique, as it enabled him to deconstruct the stereotyped mythical elements.

Being chivalrous, dominating and adventurous are some of the qualities attributed to male gender. On the other hand, the female gender is expected to be submissive, amiable, supportive and sensitive. These stereotypical portrayals in various genres like poetry, drama and novel have been ingrained in everyone's blood. By affixing such qualities, one's perception on gender gets limited forcing them to stay like a stick in a mud refusing to alter when situation demands. This narrow view cuts down all the relishing moments and fails to recognise the multi-faceted aspects in all genders.

Though the gender discrimination is slowly fading away, in this modern world one could still trace out the presence of a thin line which splits the role of sexes based on its preconceived notions. Breaking these shackles, both the genders wish to prove how good they are in accomplishing things that break the gender bias. This leads to the emergence of many female-centric genres which deconstructs the stereotyped gender discrimination. This void has created space for the budding writers like Amish Tripathi to unleash their creativity.

Centralising the diminutive characters, marginalising the protagonists, justifying the role of antagonists are some of the new vistas explored by writers. By doing this, they break the conventional narrative style which has been used for generations together. Apart from these female-centric themes, many writers derive pleasure in altering the stereotyped myth. Amish Tripathi, Devdutt Pattanaik, Kavita Kane, Anand Neelakantan, Dharamvir Bharti, and Ashwin Sanghi are some of the Indian writers who are known for retelling the Indian myths. Their unique storyline sets trap in all young minds who wish to live in that fantasy world that fulfils all their yearnings. These modern myths provide ample space for the readers to thrive and live in that comfort zone.

The Krishna Key by Ashwin Sanghi centres around the life of a serial killer who believes himself to be an incarnation of Lord Vishnu. Searching the precious stone 'Syamantaka' further augments the thrilling effect in it. Kavita Kane's *Sita's sister* focuses much on "Urmila", one of the most neglected characters in "Ramayana." The entire novel deals with the life of Urmila in Ayodhya castle. Valmiki's Ramayana is all about Ram and Sita and it never focused on Lakshman's wife "Urmila". In the advent of bringing out the brotherhood, Valmiki sacrificed the role of Mithila's younger princess. By centralising this marginalised character, Kavita Kane has weaved fourteen years of forsaken life lead by Urmila in Ayodhya castle. But she does not alter the real plot set by Valmiki.

The Ramayana is one of the famous epics in Hindu literature which deals with the life and adventures of Lord Ram. In myth, Ram is considered as the seventh incarnation of God Vishnu. His sole purpose is to assassinate Raavan and restore peace in world. To achieve this, he takes birth in the kingdom of Ayodhya and marries Sita who is the incarnation of Goddess Lakshmi. Later the story shifts to Ram's fourteen years of exile in Dandaka forest which leads to an encounter with Surpanaka and its consequences leading to Sita's abduction. Later the myth ends with Ram seeking the refuge of Hanuman to wage war against the mighty Raavan. After winning the battle, he brings back Sita and tests her chastity to prove her virtuousness. Fate again intervenes, where Sita gets deserted in the wood giving birth to her twin child Lava and Kusa. In the final years of her life, Sita lived under the protection of the sage Valmiki until the mother goddess carries her back into the earth in the celestial throne.

Amish Tripathi has deconstructed the whole myth by leaving little room for stereotyped plot structure. Both of his *Shiva Trilogy* and *Ram Chandra Series* aims at deconstructing the original Shiva Purana and Ramayana. I have chosen the first two novels in Ram Chandra Series as the primary source to reason out the ways in which Amish has deconstructed the gender bias. To affirm the equanimity between Ram and Sita, Amish Tripathi has created a similar circumstance where both failed to have a happy childhood. Ram gets condemned for King Dasarath's defeat in Karachapa war. Sita feels embarrassed to be in Mithila after Urmila's birth. In spite of all these adverse circumstances, Ram proved himself as an excellent chief of police and Sita, as an abled-prime minister of Mithila.

Both Vishwamitra and Vashista are very keen on proving that their choice is better than the other. But, one can never trace out such enmity or competency between Ram and Sita. Just like Ram, she is also obsessed with law and dharma. But Sita remains more pragmatic in certain aspects. She trespasses the boundary lines whenever the situation demands. Hiring Mara to kill Sulochan is the valid example for this. But Ram does not give room for any personal feelings or soft corners, in terms of law. He is a stern follower of law. Refusing to punish Dhenuka, living fourteen years outside the boundaries of Sapt Sindu for firing the Asuraastra are some of the crucial incidents that proves the attitude of law-abiding Ram. Sita's admiration towards Ram gets revealed in the following sentence uttered by her to Raavan. She says, "I know a man who never loses his focus, no matter how much suffering he undergoes. The greater the grief, the more righteous his response. I always thought that he would make a better Vishnu than I would. Now I know for sure." (War of Lanka 47)

In Valmiki's Ramayana, Sita gets to know Ram only after he reaches Mithila. She learns more about Ram only after the Swayamvar. "He loved her dearly because she had been given to him as a wife by his father but his love for her deepened because of her beauty and her many virtues. She loved Rama twice as much as he loved her." (The Ramayana – 98) But even before meeting Ram, Sita decided that Ram should be her life partner. Instead of going after material gain and comfort, she concentrated only on pairing with a man with whom she can struggle for the betterment of Indian nation. When Radhika explains what sort of boring person Ram is, Sita marvels at the uniqueness in him. She thinks, *"But he will probably make a good Vishnu."* (Sita 180)

In Valmiki's Ramayana, both Vishwamitra and King Janak played a vital role in arranging the marriage between Ram and Sita. But Sita pressed on her marriage only here. Her intention to win the hands of Ram gets explicitly revealed in the following statements, "Sita was actively managing the arrangements. She had convinced Vishwamitra to somehow get Ram to Mithila for the swayamvar." (Sita 185) She was the one who suggested marrying Ram which remains agreeable to Vishwamitra. Because he thought this would enable him to have a hand on Vashishta's favourite student "Ram".

Just like in Valmiki's portrayal Ram remains loyal and law-abiding in the perception of Amish Tripathi too. His love for dharma aids Ram to reconcile with his father. King Dasarath admires his son's love towards dharma and other moral principles. When it comes to Dharma, Ram never hesitates to let out his opinion. He says, "Nobody is above the law, Father. None can be more powerful that dharma." (Ram 130) In all these incidents, one can find the ways in which Amish Tripathi has deconstructed the gender discrimination found in the ancient myth. Like Ram, Sita is also good in martial skills. While King Janak remains a voracious reader, it becomes the sole responsibility of Sunaina to govern the kingdom and bring up Sita at the same time. When it comes to Mithila, Sunaina and Sita played a major role in administrative works.

In common, marriage alters the general course of life. It brings many changes in the life of two persons who step into a new life without knowing what their future holds. But through Ram and Sita Amish Tripathi has bought out the image of an ideal couple who never intrude the privacy of others without their consent. Knowing well that Sita is the next Vishnu in Vishwamitra's perception, Ram never forced her to admit it. But Ram patiently waited for her to let it out. He says, "I have known you for years. Heard so many of your ideas. You will make a great Vishnu. I will be proud of you." (Sita 331) In the above said lines, one could see how Ram and Sita on the well-being of others. Each want the other to get the title of Vishnu and do good for the Indian nation. Administering the Kingdom, defeating the opponents, planning all the battle strategies are some aspects in which only the male gender plays a key role. But Sita excels in all these and proves herself to be a better person in all situations. In spite of all these efficient qualities, she always remains humble and despises hovering behind fame that she does not deserve.

When it comes to age, men always go behind women who are younger to them. In the institution of marriage, they expect their life partner to be younger, beautiful and innocent in worldly aspects. To deconstruct this difference in age, Amish has portrayed Sita as a girl who is five years elder to Ram. But this age difference does not remain odd in the eyes of any.

However gruesome the crime may be, Ram focused not only in punishing the victim, but he also wants it to be carried out in accordance with dharmic principles. Though he wants to kill Dhenuka, he could not do it, as he is a minor. So, he inflicts pain on himself for having not safeguarding his sister, Roshini in her excruciating moment. But Sita remains more pragmatic, as she does some unethical deed to get things done. All she needs is a quick, practical solution to lift up all the hurdles in her path. Killing a boy in the slum, assassinating Sulochan by hiring Mara are some of the incidents that brings out the revolting spirit in Sita. Whether the outcome of her deed is good or bad, she always focused on implementing her plans. In the real myth, Sita doubted Lakshman when he refuses to help Ram and she even questions him for having developed evil intentions towards her. This could be seen in the following lines uttered by Sita, "You followed Rama, who is vulnerable and without protection, into the forest only so that you could have me!" (The Ramayana 274) But in this abduction scene, Amish Tripathi has picturised Sita as a warrior. Because Amish Tripathi knows that the modern Sita never doubts or easily gets swayed by any luring objects. She tried her level best to protect Jatayu and other Malayaputra soldiers from Raavan's troops. As they are outnumbered, it becomes impossible for her to win them hands down.

She proved herself to be an able Vishnu, by fighting for herself whenever the situation demands. Malayaputras and Vishwamitra sided with Sita, while Vayuputras and Vashishta focused on Ram. Their bitter enmity and thirst for power does not get into the veins of Ram and Sita. They are ready to sacrifice the title of Vishnu and strive for the betterment of their motherland. Vashishta chooses Ram for being a stern believer in dharma. But Vishwamitra chooses Sita, only after knowing that she is the daughter of Vedavati. Because he knows that by choosing Sita, he can have a control on Raavan who will never hurt the daughter of Vedavati, his Kanyakumari.

In the perception of Amish Tripathi gaining the title of Vishnuhood is not an easy task. A person's karma and their ardent belief in law and dharma makes them worthy enough to receive the title of Vishnu. Both Vishwamitra and Vashishta chooses Ram and Sita after analysing their calibre in various stages. Vishwamitra believes in Sita because of her birth mother, Vedavati utilising this he can set a trap for Raavan. Vishwamitra is the only person who knows the bondage between Raavan and Vedavati. When Sita gets abducted, all are worried about her well-being. But only Vishwamitra knows that Raavan would never dare to touch or harm the daughter of Vedavati. Raavan's unrequited love plays a key role in altering his own fate.

On the other hand, Vashishta chooses Ram for his love towards law and dharma. He remains unbiased in passing sentences, irrespective of their background and social influence. Even Sita admires this quality in Ram, as she herself chooses illegal ways to accomplish her desires. In Valmiki's "Ramayana", Raavan's intention to abduct Sita is purely based on lust. Surpanaka's provoking words kindled his desire to obtain Sita. This could be traced in the following words uttered by Surpanaka to Raavan. She says, "Rama also has a beautiful wife named Sita. Large-eyed and delicate, she is the princess of Videha and she is the best of all women. Not even among the gods, the gandharvis, the yaksis or the kinnaris have I seen a woman as lovely as this one." (The Ramayana 261) But Amish Tripathi has deconstructed this stereotyped concept to bring out the goodness within Raavan. Deep within his sadistic nature, one can trace out the presence of tender heart that gains solace by clutching the phalanges of Vedavati.

Thus, the striking conflict in gender identity vanishes in the modern myth narrated by Amish Tripathi. This modern myth has given a new dimension by shifting its focus from the conventional style. Many writers are keen on deconstructing the basic ideologies in myth which gives much priority to male characters. By altering the stereotyped narration, the writer has succeeded in making the story even more interesting and agreeable without reducing the characters' worthiness. Though the real myth is the base, Amish Tripathi's passion to deconstruct the gender discrimination gets explicitly seen in all his works.

References

- Sattar, Arshia. *Valmiki: The Ramayana.* Penguin books. 1996.
- Tripathi, Amish. *Ram.* Westland publishers. 2015.
- Tripathi, Amish. *Sita.* Westland publishers. 2017.
- Tripathi, Amish. War of Lanka. HaperCollins publishers. 2022.

---

[1]**R. Lavanya,** Head and Assistant Professor in English at VHNSNCollege (Autonomous), Virudhunagar. Interested in Indian Writing in English and Feminist literature. My passion is to educate and enlighten the budding generation with abundant knowledge.

[2]**Dr. K. Muthurajan,** Associate Professor in English at VHNSN College (Autonomous), Virudhunagar. Interested in Indian Writing in English and American Literature. Through teaching, I wish to instill virtues in budding minds.

• • •

CHAPTER XXI

Gender Exclusion to Inclusion: Overcoming Terror with the Power of Self-Defense in Vipin Das's Movie Jaya Jaya Jaya Jaya Hey

Sincy Davis

Research Scholar, Mahatma Gandhi University, Kerala

Abstract

Violence against women stems from terror. The age-old belief that women's bodies are weaker than men's strengthens this fear. The current increase in rapes, domestic violence, and dowry deaths reveals that women are afraid to fight against their oppressors.Women should consider the significance of attaining physical strength and confidence at this juncture. Gender theories explain gender as socially constructed. Physical feminism focuses on the emancipation of women by strengthening their minds and bodies. Martial arts training may be a better choice for women to defend themselves against men's physical superiority as it can be practiced by anyone regardless of gender. This article studies the capacity of women to challenge their oppressors and use physical resistance through martial arts with the support of the latest Malayalam movie, Jaya Jaya Jaya Jaya Hey. As the story unravels, Jaya, the main character, endures gender exclusion both in education and in the institution of marriage. However, towards the middle of the story, Jaya's transformation from a silent to a self-confident woman with the support of martial arts becomes visible, which helps her to overcome the terror she had in her mind. The capacity of women to shift their living surroundings from a gender exclusive to a gender-inclusive one with body strength and mind power is also the focus of the study.

Keywords: Physical feminism, Martial Arts, Body, Gender inclusion, Violence

---

Terror is the root cause of violence against women, depending on power differences. Now the question is, Is there any remedy to this? What makes women more vulnerable to attacks from men is their inability to find a solution to their problems. So, the answer to the question mentioned above is women themselves have to find a remedy to their suffering. At first, they need to tackle the power differences to gain mental and physical strength. Physical feminism focuses on strengthening and emancipating women from men's violence by embracing their physical capacity. Women can utilize their mind power attained through self-defense to overcome men's aggression (Noel 20). Physical feminism also highlights women's capacity to challenge societal gender norms, which promotes women's subordination (Noel 21). Martial arts can be considered one such platform for women to empower themselves. It can also alter the beliefs about the bodily relationships between men and women constructed in sexual and parental contexts (Maor 40). The practical ways of empowering women through martial arts, as illustrated by Vipin Das in his recent movie Jaya Jaya Jaya Jaya Hey, is the central concern of this study.

As the film opens, the main protagonist Jayabharathi catches the audience's attention mainly through the different patterns of gender exclusion she suffers, be it at home or in society. Jaya conforms to the practices of a traditional Kerala girl who accepts everything even though she has strong disagreements with many of them in her mind. Not only does she receive verbal attacks but also, she bears both mental and physical blows. She appears as a weak figure, silently enduring all the pains that come her way. In the movie's first part, Jaya embodies women's vulnerability. The male members of her family force Jaya to learn something out of her choice, although she procures a chance to pursue higher studies in Anthropology, her dream subject. Jaya's husband, Rajesh, a short-tempered person, utilizes every opportunity to abuse her physically. Jaya endures the first blow upon her nose from her over-possessive boyfriend, thus leading to committing an early marriage. Married life doesn't prove a haven for her, whose saga of agony continues. Jaya grew up in a patriarchal male-dominated society where male figures controlled every decision. Jaya somehow manages to draw permission for online education, which she employs brilliantly to overcome the terror in her and, thus, her husband's brutality.

Gender-based violence occurs commonly in different communities worldwide irrespective of being a developed or an underdeveloped country—also, the reasons for that vary. However, in a country like India, it is most often linked to age-old beliefs, prejudices, and customs. Society not only convinces women that they are weak but also makes them weak by differentiating masculine and feminine ideals and forcing them to meet those (Roth and Basow 249). Violence approach women in various forms, such as physical, sexual, emotional, financial, social, and intellectual (Sharma and Gupta 114- 115). Women also undergo violence in the form of denial of education, health facilities, and reproductive rights (Sharma and Gupta114-115). The movie Jaya Jaya Jaya Jaya Hey shows Jaya facing most of these kinds of violence. Her husband's constant verbal and physical attacks weaken Jaya emotionally and physically. However, Jaya was not ready to repeatedly fall prey to all these, although her parents forced her to accept every pain silently, which they regarded as a common rule for women. Her decision to find a way out of her struggle culminates in undergoing online martial arts training. Her determination to overcome her subservience becomes apparent as the audience watches the independent training sessions in the bathroom or on the terrace. Jaya kept it a secret until the right time. She doesn't even give a hint to her husband about it, as she wants to ground him with a single mass kick. Jaya's act reveals this fact as she transforms from a slender, vulnerable figure into an overpowering empress. The audience and her husband are startled at her first attack. A well-disciplined self-defense training can empower women's bodies and challenge men's invincibility (Thompson 354).

Martial arts training for women can help outwit male dominance over them, thus granting a sense of confidence in their physical selves. Women's change to the role of a training partner rather than a mere sex partner can help wipe out the gender exclusion they undergo in marital life. The fact, as mentioned earlier, can very well be illustrated by studying Jaya's situation in Jaya Jaya Jaya Jaya Hey. Viewers get an idea of the forthcoming troubles in Jaya's life on the very day of her marriage, which is brought forth by the unnecessary cries of her relatives while sending her to her husband's house. She is shocked at the sight of the broken table and helplessly places the lighted lantern at her first entry to the house. Rajesh's house name Raj Bhavan focuses on his dominance in the domestic world. Everyone at home is under his control, and no one dares to question his wrong behavior even though they are well aware of it—Rajesh's attitude sprouts from society's false perception of men's predominant and women's subordinate roles. Jaya provides complete respect for her husband and in-laws in the early stage of her married life. When she finds the difficulty of her mother-in-law struggling to prepare the same breakfast her son likes, Jaya takes her turn and tries to make something new for her husband. For this silly reason, she receives most of the blows from him. Each time after a physical attack, Rajesh takes Jaya to a restaurant and mockingly asks what she wants and never orders anything of her choice. Rajesh's behavior can be attributed to his decision not wanting to give her the slightest chance to be his equal. Jaya reaches a stage where she can no longer suffer anything more. Once when she was lazily lying on the sofa with her mobile phone, Rajesh arrived and angrily tried to grab that phone. At this moment, she reacts with full power kicking him to the edge of the room. In this instance, for the first time, Rajesh is identifiable as a terrified person. He never expected such a tremendous strike from her side. An abrupt stillness is identifiable in him after such aggressive behavior from Jaya. The first sign of Jaya's success is noticeable in this instance.

Self–defense training can help women understand their value, gain self-confidence, overcome fear, satisfy their physical capacity, be aware of sexism, and have a sense of liberty (Channon 8). However, like any other field that depends upon body strength, women need to increase their performance level and physical capacity with formal practice sessions to gain excellence in martial arts and to erase the power difference between men and women. In the movie, Jaya Jaya Jaya Jaya Hey Jaya undergoes such practice sessions to overcome the barriers of gender exclusion that she experiences in marriage. With a single powerful stroke, Jaya could transfer the terror feeling in her into Rajesh's mind. Rajesh is embarrassed to reveal the physical damage his wife caused him, even to his family and friends. That much is the impact it has upon him. Instead, he decides to fight back. Through continuous practice, he, too, gains some courage and tries his best to win over Jaya in the fight. Anyway, the mind power received by facing the harsh realities of life is enough for Jaya to outwit her opponent. Now, for the second time, Rajesh is grounded by Jaya, shocking the sensibilities of his mother and sister, who suddenly returns home.

Meanwhile, Jaya also faces emotional blows from Rajesh's cousin and mother. However, she was not ready to accept everything silently. Instead, Jaya questions them back, pointing out the pains she had to endure in marital life. Still, she cannot find solace in anyone as they blame her unnecessarily. Even though everyone isolates Jaya, she adjusts well to the situation with the self-confidence acquired through martial arts skills. This film also foregrounds a clear case of reproductive injustice or violence against women's reproductive rights. Later in the movie, Rajesh approaches Jaya cunningly in the guise of a loving husband to outwit her sexually. Jaya never understands his plan until she becomes pregnant. When Jaya realizes that it was a forced pregnancy brought forth by Rajesh to exert his control, she becomes enfeebled, leading to a miscarriage. She regains her strength, leaves the hospital alone, and never returns to Rajesh's place. Jaya made such a firm decision mainly by the self-esteem obtained through martial arts training. Jaya attains complete autonomy towards the end of the movie when she secures herself financially as a poultry dealer. She also fights her husband's workers, who come with bad intentions to threaten her poultry business.

Unlike the other female figures in the movie, Jaya tries to build a different story for herself: not of silence and cowardice but of courage and power. She emerges as a symbol of hope and freedom for the entire women's community. Jaya's parents and relatives always wanted to keep her in a safe zone and never tried to mold her into a courageous girl. During her childhood, Jaya climbed up the trees along with the boys. Jaya's uncle reprimands her instantly for climbing the trees like the boys. Deep in her consciousness, Jaya wanted to be equal to the boys, and she felt nothing wrong with it. The thought of power equalization she tried to attain through martial arts in later life was within her from the beginning stages of her life. Anyway, Jaya's true identity lay hidden deep within.

Jaya had decisions about her studies and carrier, which she had to sacrifice to please society and her family. When Jaya had to bear a decisive blow from her boyfriend, nobody questioned that person; instead, she faced victim blaming. Instead, they take it as a chance to wind up her studies and thus force an early marriage. She has no choice but to play the role destined for her by her parents. However, Jaya didn't take it too seriously until her marriage. Rajesh's aggressiveness forces her to make an independent decision about her life as she knows she cannot expect any support from her parents. Usually, in movies, when a woman faces troubles, she gets mental help from her intimate friends. Jaya's case is far different from this as she suffers all pains alone. She understands the necessity of attaining body strength and mind power to solve her problems. Physical abuse can be outwitted powerfully only by employing a reciprocal physical attack and nothing else, Jaya learns. Keen observation and hard work help her to develop mastery over Taekwon-Do, a Korean form of martial arts.

Media often portray rape and domestic violence, arousing the audience's sympathy. Women's depiction as helpless creatures is not new for the viewers. Anyway, such a portrayal has brought no commendable growth in erasing gender exclusion from society. However, Jaya Jaya Jaya Jaya Hey is a praiseworthy movie on account of its rare portrait of a woman as a fearless and heroic figure. Malayalam films rarely picture women's capacity to resist assault. In that case, this movie can certainly be a thought provoker for people who regard women as susceptible to assaults. Women themselves have to take charge of their issues and find a solution rather than waiting for someone to manage and make them worse. Society often compels women to stick to the traditional stereotypically feminine traits such as being non-aggressive, dependent, passive, submissive, and indecisive. This benefits man with a chance to exert his power upon her. However, women's opportunity to undergo training sessions with men in martial arts can certainly awaken their consciousness into awareness about their hidden powers. Everyone, regardless of gender or body size, can utilize martial arts skills as it is not dependent on body strength (Noel 23). While most other sports requiring body strength, like cricket, rugby, and others, classify them into separate teams based on sex, martial arts doesn't (Noel 23).Hence undoubtedly, this can provide a firm ground for women to defeat their oppressors. In Jaya Jaya Jaya Jaya Hey, it is interesting to note the gradual development in Jaya's attitude about life while practicing Taekwon-Do. She manages to escape her role as a subservient wife to an independent woman.

Gender exclusion and violence that women live through arise mainly in a patriarchal society where males dominate women's rights. Rajesh's character in the movie Jaya Jaya Jaya Jaya Hey is analogous to such persons who disagree with gender equality. Rajesh always looks for a view from a male relative in place of seeking his mother's opinion. He cannot tolerate any rise in a female's voice in his house and brilliantly keeps them under his control. Rajesh comes down to Jaya's level or below only after she throws him away with a big kick. He is frightened at the sudden power reversal in their relationship. Society regards women as passive beings and hence disagrees with their opportunity to undergo self-defense training (Hollander 12). Popular media also repeatedly portray women's passivity. Antiviolence campaigns and protests for women's rights often fail to bring about a significant change in the situation. However, good self-defense trainers always encourage women and condemn society when they fail to react to violence (Hollander 10). Through self-defense training, women transform their weak bodies into strong ones like men as a step toward gender inclusivity. Women who take the initiative to build self-efficacy by undoing societal barriers must be well appreciated. Vipin Das, the director of the movie Jaya JayaJayaJaya Hey, with his portrayal of the character Jayabharathi honors womanhood and provides a visual treat of women empowerment. He shifts from the media's usual focus on women's weaknesses. Jaya Jaya Jaya Jaya Hey completely utilizes the media's influence on the mass to accomplish its mission to eliminate the phenomenon of gender exclusion. Jaya's decision to find a space for herself reveals a woman's capacity to expunge gender inequality. With her change to the role of a businesswoman and the power attained from martial arts, Jaya builds a gender-inclusive world of her own.

References

- Channon, Alex. "Martial Arts Studies and the Sociology of Gender: Theory, Research, and Pedagogical Application." The Martial Arts Studies Reader, edited by Paul Bowman. London: Rowman & Littlefield International, 2018.
- Hollander, Jocelyn A. "The Roots of Resistance to Women's Self-Defense."
- Violence Against Women, vol.XX, no.X, 10 Feb. 2009.SAGE doi:10.1177/1077801209331407

- Jaya Jaya Jaya Jaya Hey. Directed by Vipin Das, performances by Darshana Rajendran and Basil Joseph, Cheers Entertainments, 2022.
- Kuehnast, Kathleen and Danielle Robertson. Gender Inclusive Framework and Theory: A Guide for Turning Theory into Practice, United States Institute of Peace, 2018. www. USIP. org
- Maor, Maya. "Fighting Gender Stereotypes: Women's Participation in the Martial Arts, Physical Feminism and Social Change." Martial Arts Studies, vol.7,pp 36-48. doi:org/ 10.18573/mas.56
- Noel, HarmoniJoie. "Undoing Gendered Power Relations Through Martial Arts?" International Journal of Social Inquiry, vol.2, no.2, 2009, pp 17-37.
- Rentschler, Carrie A. "Women's Self-Defense: Physical Education for Everyday Life." Women's Studies Quarterly, vol.27, no.1/2, 1999, pp 152-161. JSTOR, http://www.jstor.org/ stable/40003408. Accessed 21 Dec. 2022.
- Roth, Amanda and Susan A.Basow. "Femininity, Sports, and Feminism: Developing a Theory of Physical Liberation."Journal of Sport and Social Issues, vol.28, no.3, Aug.2004, pp 245-265. SAGE. doi:10.1177/0193723504266990
- Sharma B.R and Manisha Gupta. "Gender Based Violence in India: A Never Ending Phenomenon." Journal of International Women's Studies, vol.6, no.1, Nov.2004, pp 114-123. https://vc.bridgew.edu/jiws/vol6/iss1/8
- Thompson, Martha E. "Empowering Self-Defense Training." Violence Against Women, vol.20, no.3, 2014, pp 351-359. doi:10.1177/1077801214526051

Sincy Davis, is a researcher in English literature at Mahatma Gandhi University, India. She has published articles based on Ecocriticism in an international journal. A passionate lover of English literature with seven years of experience teaching in the field at various colleges under Mahatma Gandhi University. Being a postgraduate in English literature and Microbiology, she has presented research papers at national level in both the disciplines.

• • •

215

CHAPTER XXII

The Inclusion of Genderqueer in Malayalam Films Chanthupott and Mumbai Police

Sruthi Merin Mathew

Research Scholar, English Department, School of Social Sciences and Languages, Vellore Institute of Technology

Abstract

Films which are one of the most influential cultural modes of expression always have had a significant role in conditioning the audiences' minds. This paper critically looks into the instances in the Malayalam films which incorporates queer community in their narratives. It would question the 'normalizing' attitudes often seen in those films which depict the lives of the queer community as an aberration from the 'normal' standards, thereby, throwing some light upon the serious issues faced by the queer community resulting from such 'normalizing' attitudes often seen in the Malayalam films. The inclusion of queer characters in the films like Chanthupott (2005) and Mumbai Police (2013) are depicted in different or to an extent in contrasting levels. Even though, both these films try to integrate gender inclusivity within their narratives, the question arises when one ponders upon the fact whether these representations and articulation of queer identity could show some justice to the queer community who are often underrepresented or misrepresented. As many of the audience is so receptive to the notions portrayed through the films, such representations should be carried out sensibly and realistically.

Keywords: inclusion, queer

Films which are one of the most influential cultural modes of expression always have had a significant role in conditioning the audiences' minds. This paper critically looks into the instances in the Malayalam films which incorporates queer community in their narratives. It would question the 'normalizing' attitudes often seen in those films which depict the lives of the queer community as an aberration from the 'normal' standards, thereby, throwing some light upon the serious issues faced by the queer community resulting from such 'normalizing' attitudes often seen in the Malayalam films. The inclusion of queer characters in the films like *Chanthupott* (2005) and *Mumbai Police* (2013) are depicted in different or to an extent in contrasting levels. Even though, both these films try to integrate gender inclusivity within their narratives, the question arises when one ponders upon the fact whether these representations and articulation of queer identity could show some justice to the queer community who are often underrepresented or misrepresented. As many of the audience is so receptive to the notions portrayed through the films, such representations should be carried out sensibly and realistically.

Chanthupott is one of those popular films that despite its effort to represent an effeminate character has failed at the same as the depiction was not at all justifiable. Rather it reinforced the patriarchal view of the heteronormativity of the society. It is a 2005 film directed by Lal Jose and written by Benny P. Nayarambalam. The plot revolves around the main character Radha Krishnan who is an effeminate person. He is brought up like a girl by his grandmother. He is scorned by society for his mannerisms and dressing styles. Despite the fact that the film chronicles the story of a transvestite person, it portrays the character as a 'deviant' from society, therefore 'othering' the character. "Crossdressing by men was casually incorporated into the script as superficial additions to provide laughter" (Raj et al. 55). After the release of this film, the tendency to mock effeminate individuals by calling them 'Chanthupott' was very common in Kerala, and the very same word was used to harass transgender people too. Throughout the film, there is this continuous compulsion on Radha to live like a macho man. He is often ridiculed by society for his gender expression. "It comes as no surprise that mainstream cinematic representations in the Malayalam tradition emphasize the dominant heterosexual or heteronormative order and that any articulation of queer is represented with taboos or become an object of humour, sarcasm or ridicule" (Sreedevi 2). Radha is denied agency over his own gender identity, as he is told to prove his virility by conforming to heteronormative ideals. The conservative social milieu is further re-established as the film narrative continues to take an unapologetic stance towards anything that is 'deviant' from the heteronormative tradition. The filmmaker's deliberate endeavour to conform to the audience's popular expectations that eschew other sexual patterns is well mirrored in the film which successfully places Radha in a traditionally masculine world; thereby upholding and normalizing heterosexuality.

Radha who is a dance teacher is portrayed as a cross-dresser who wears make-up unlike other men in his fishermen community. He is depicted as a person who is always in the company of girls and as a person who tries to talk like a girl. This 'feminine' behaviour is often evident in his interaction with the men as Radha's body language manifests the cis-feminine characteristics of shyness and caution while doing the same. "Divakaran, the father of the central character, tries to bring out the pain and humiliation of having a progeny laughed at by society" (Prabhakaran and Poovathingal 319). Radha is frequently scolded by his father for his effeminate mannerisms. Things escalate when his mother also asks him to show his manliness in front of all those people on that shore. Weeping, she tells him that he must prove himself as a man and that women should desire him. The film then shows a complete shift in Radha's attitude, as all of a sudden, he focuses on his 'manly' features. The scene where he tries to fix his moustache in order to appear more masculine is an example of this. He then develops feelings for Malu, which is reciprocated by the latter. The heterosexual norm is re-established when Radha falls in love with a female; later on, firmly securing him as a heterosexual husband towards the end of the plot. He is outcasted by the people of his shore, as Komban Kumaran, a macho-man (who adores Malu) finds out their relationship and informs about it to Malu's father who is the astrologer and chief of their community. Kumaran and his gang try to kill him. Radha is eventually rescued by Freddy, who epitomizes 'masculine' features. Radha's identity as a transvestite is appropriated by Freddy and his sister Rosie. They restrain him from doing any domestic chores that are often deemed as women's jobs. He is forced to dress like a macho man and to behave like one. "If you are a man, live like one; don't dishonour others with your effeminate behaviourism" (Jose 01: 23:21). This is one of the many comments articulated by the character Rosie, which shows that any disruption in the heteronormative sentiments is right away 'corrected' by the society, without even addressing the real issue at stake.

The denouement of the film shows how Radha comes back to his shore as a 'changed' person; who has transformed himself into a man with the expected masculine characteristics; wearing pants and shirts and without any make-up. He is also depicted as going to fish with the other fishermen which again reinforces the patriarchal notion of confined gender roles. Throughout the film, there is a desperate desire to standardise the identity preferences of every community and to overemphasize the notion of marital bliss (arising from a marriage between a male and a female) that always triumphs. The villagers accept him as they see the transformed Radha who has proved his potency by impregnating Malu (who has now given birth to a boy child). The filmmaker is thus reiterating the need of appropriating any divergent behaviour from the cis-heteronormative standards. In the fight scene towards the end of the film, "we notice that he has shed most of his effeminate traits. This represents the way he is transformed to the stereotype"

(Prabhakaran and Poovathingal 322). The mirroring of the social prejudices predominant in the Indian society fades the queer themes in the narrative "since the films bind one's sexual preferences to their moral and psychological well-being" (Raj et al. 51). The fear of deviating from the heteronormative tradition is visible in the way the narrative presents artistic manifestations. This film thus consciously positions Radha in a traditional world of heteronormativity.

Mumbai Police is a Malayalam film directed by Roshan Andrews and written by Bobby and Sanjay. It was a commercially successful film in Kerala with its pathbreaking attempt to disrupt from the normal tendency of portraying a heterosexual hero, thereby making it the first Indian film with a gay hero (The New Indian Express). The question arises when one ponders upon the thought whether the film was able to represent the queer sensibilities in a justifiable manner. From one perspective, the respective film permitted "throwing homophobia on the table for discussion" (The New Indian Express) and bringing up a much-forbidden topic on the main screen. On the other hand, it did not adhere to queer aesthetics due to certain loopholes within the narrative.

This crime-thriller film revolves around the lives of three police officers who were referred as the 'Mumbai Police' as they served in the Mumbai counter terrorism in their earlier life. The narrative begins in media res and follows a non-linear structure. The main character ACP Antony Moses meets with an accident which leads to partial memory loss. He was at the verge of revealing the name of the culprit of ACP Aryan John Jacob's murder just before the accident. The story is about Antony reinvestigating the case to track the truth behind his best friend's demise. In the end, it is exposed that the murderer was none other than the main investigator himself. But what led him to do this brutal act? That is the crucial suspense of the film. Aryan finds out that Antony was a homosexual and threatens to expose his closeted sexuality which leads the latter to kill Aryan. The storyline seems unproblematic at first glance.

Even if the film was daring in portraying gay love, the confusion arises as the crucial element in the film (fear of coming out) is used as an element to evoke the shock element in the audience. It does not cater to the queer sensibilities as any such thoughts are right away discarded as one of the reasons for the criminal tendency of the protagonist. The film is carefully crafted within the rigid patriarchal and heteronormative structure positioned in a male-centred world which does not cause any discomfort to the (homophobic) audience. When Aryan finds out that Antony is gay, his outburst parallels with the heterosexual expectations of the general public consensus. He tells Antony that he would never visit him again and goes to an extent saying that he's now doubtful whether Antony had 'wrong' intentions on him too. Aryan even articulates that Antony's criminal tendency is the consequence of his 'deviant' sexuality. He calls his gay nature as a sign of unmanliness and identifies his violent macho personality in the public as a mask to hide this 'weakness', i.e., his sexuality. Thus, "this film subverts the portrayal of gayness as less than masculine" (Raj et al. 51). Right after Aryan walks out of Antony's home, the audience is able to observe the tensions that Antony and his gay partner goes through, as exposing their sexual identity would ruin their public self. This fear of being 'othered' in a heterosexual society or in simple terms, the fear of coming out urges the protagonist to kill his closest friend. They dreaded that it would end up their career, consequently, allowing the society to tag them as the 'outcasts'-"The emotionally charged scene towards the end of the movie in which the couple confronts Aryan echoes how terribly they want to be closeted for the 'coming out' would risk their personal as well as public life" (Babu 14).

The way in which the duality of the protagonist's personality is interweaved within the narrative as the Antony Moses before the memory loss (let it be Antony A) and the Moses after the memory loss (Antony B) is demarcated with each of the selves exhibiting different sexual inclinations is quite problematic. Sexuality is not something that could be forgotten and towards the end of the film, one is able to discern how Antony B angrily reacts to his gay partner with disgust and discomfort. He throws him out of his house and the camera then focuses merely on Antony B, inevitably negating the existence of his partner. This in itself is an act of 'othering' queer sexualities as it fails to incorporate the queer perspective. Antony B is completely estranged from Antony A. Despite being able to remember all the skills that he had once, he forgets his sexuality and his character is positioned in a world that conforms to the heteronormative expectations. Antony A is aggressive, stubborn, barbaric and inconsiderate whereas Antony B is more humanitarian and considerate. "The ideology of heteronormativity further creates and disseminates stereotypical images of homosexuals with all the deviant attributes" (Babu 12). Thus, Antony A becomes the villain of the plot, whereas Antony B becomes the hero who unveils the truth of his former self's brutality. "The movie ends with Moses in his present condition as a heterosexual person completely acceptable to the society. It ends as if the past is immoral and a time that should not happen anymore" (Babu 14).

Both of the films, *Chanthupott* and *Mumbai Police* point out the disappointing fact that any kind of act or behaviour that is an aberration to the heterosexual standards are labelled as deviant and anyone who unfollows that standard is bound to be ostracised. The way in which the queer community is portrayed or their characterisation in these film narratives further portray their identity as something undefined and blurred. Instead of giving a thrust upon the mainstream society by constructing an identity for the queer community, these films uphold and normalise heterosexuality as it fails to address their concerns properly. Instead, they are 'othered' in some or another way and strikingly alienated from the society. "Representation of sexuality in mainstream Indian cinema is circumscribed to be heteronormative, more specifically to cater to the (perverted) sexual fantasies of the cisgender heterosexual male" (Chatterjee 95). Setting limitations would distort rather than reveal the lived experiences of the queer community. Instead of empowering the queer community, the visibility of queer concerns in a distorted way would endanger them making them subject to increased discrimination. Sanjay, one of the scriptwriters of *Mumbai Police* in an interview says that "the second Antony Moses who loses his memory is more of a normal man" (George and Sreekumar). The use of the word 'normal' here portrays any other sexualities as abnormal. Lal Jose, the director of *Chanthupott* justifies his misrepresentation of the transvestite protagonist in one of his interviews (Joseph and Jayarajan, The News Minute). Both of the films were commercially successful mainly because it "carefully places the queer subtext as an undertone to normalise and validate heterosexual order and norms" (Raj et al., 2018, p. 43). Even though, these films were released before the decriminalisation of Section 377 of the IPC and The Transgender Persons (Protection of Rights) Act, the misrepresentation or lack of representation cannot be vindicated.

The majority of the Malayalam psyche is socialised from birth to accept heterosexual thoughts and actions. The films have the potential to influence the view of the majority of the audience. Therefore, the misrepresentation of the queer community in films is actually worsening their situation. "This pervasiveness of the heteronormative practices and the consequent othering of other identities prevents a sympathetic response to homosexuality from the world of cultural narratives" (Raj et al. 46). Rather than portraying the queer characters as an anomaly to the 'mainstream' society, the film narratives should challenge the convenient exclusion and absence of acts that dismantle heteronormativity and breach the standard gender boundaries.

References

- Babu, Alaka T. "'Regime of the Normal': Heteronormativity and Queer Identity in the Movie Mumbai Police." *Quest Journals*, vol. 9, no. 3, 6 Mar. 2021, pp. 12-16, www.questjournals.org/ . Accessed 3 Jan. 2023.

- *Chanthupott*. Directed by Lal Jose, performances by Dileep. Lal creations, 2005. YouTube, https://youtu.be/KKCKwrBFX7I.
- Chatterjee, Hiya. "Bodies in Transition: Exploring Queer Sexualities in Indian Cinema." *Sanglap: Journal of Literary and Cultural Inquiry*, vol. 07, no. 02, 2021, pp. 95-119.
- George, Anjana, and Priya Sreekumar. "M'town goes offbeat, 'My Life Partner' and 'Odum Raja Aadum Rani' deal with homosexuality." *Deccan Chronicle*, [Kochi], 4 May 2014, www.deccanchronicle.com/140504/entertainment-mollywood/article/m%E2%80%99town-goes-offbeat-my-life-partner-and-odum-raja-aadum-rani/. Accessed 4 Jan. 2023.
- Joseph, Neethu, and Sreedevi Jayarajan. "Queer activists slam Lal Jose for defending problematic 2005 film 'Chanthupottu'." *The News Minute*, 15 Nov. 2019, www.thenewsminute.com/article/queer-activists-slam-lal-jose-defending-problematic-2005-film-chanthupottu-112378. Accessed 2 Jan. 2013.
- K, Vijesh C. "8 years of 'Mumbai Police': When Prithviraj-Rosshan Andrrews combo made Indian cinema's first gay hero." *The New Indian Express*, 28 May 2020, www.newindianexpress.com/galleries/entertainment/2020/may/28/8-years-of-mumbai-police-when-prithviraj-rosshan-andrrews-combo-made-indian-cinemasfirst-gay-he-102876--12.html. Accessed 6 Jan. 2022.
- *Mumbai Police*. Directed by Roshan Andrews, performances by Prithviraj. Central Pictures, 2013. Disney Hotstar.
- Prabhakaran, Roshni, and Nithya Poovathingal. "Masculinizing Radha: The Politics of Representation in Chandupott." *Language in India*, vol. 13, no. 8, 2013, pp. 318-325, www.languageinindia.com. Accessed 19 Dec. 2022.
- Raj, Sony Jalarajan, et al. "On the Margins of Heterosexuality! Representation of Queerness in Malayalam Cinema." *Chalachithra Sameeksha*, vol. 1, no. 8, 2018, pp. 40-59, www.researchgate.net/publication/327164196_On_the_Margins_of_eterosexuality_Representation_of_Queerness_in_Malayalam_Cinema.

Accessed 23 Dec. 2022.

- Sreedevi, T.K. (2016). "'Opting-out': the cinematic representation of hijra in Santhosh Souparnika's Ardhanaari." (2012). *Reconstruction: Studies in Contemporary Culture*, vol. 16, no. 2, 2012, https://link.gale.com/apps/doc/A490983395/AONE?u=anon~7d5ada13&sid=googleScholar&xid=ee84a989. Accessed 13 May. 2022.

Sruthi Merin Mathew, is a doctoral candidate in English Literature from the School of Social Sciences and Languages, Vellore Institute of Technology, Vellore. Her research looks into various aspects of transgender identities. She has completed her Master's degree from St. Joseph's University, Bengaluru and her Bachelor's degree from Mar Ivanios College, Thiruvananthapuram.

• • •

Leave no one behind (LNOB) is the central, transformative promise of the 2030 Agenda for Sustainable Development and its Sustainable Development Goals (SDGs). It represents the unequivocal commitment of all UN Member States to eradicate poverty in all its forms, end discrimination and exclusion, and reduce the inequalities and vulnerabilities that leave people behind and undermine the potential of individuals and of humanity as a whole.

~The **United Nations**